Lives of the Voice

LIVES
of the
VOICE

An Essay on Closeness

HANS ULRICH GUMBRECHT

STANFORD UNIVERSITY PRESS
Stanford, California

Stanford University Press
Stanford, California

English edition © 2025 by the Board of Trustees of the Leland Stanford Junior University. All rights reserved.

Published by arrangement with Suhrkamp Verlag AG Berlin. All other rights reserved by and controlled through Suhrkamp Verlag AG Berlin.

No part of this book may be reproduced or transmitted in any form or by any means, electronic or mechanical, including photocopying and recording, or in any information storage or retrieval system, without the prior written permission of Stanford University Press.

Library of Congress Cataloging-in-Publication Data
Names: Gumbrecht, Hans Ulrich, author.
Title: Lives of the voice : an essay on closeness / Hans Ulrich Gumbrecht.
Description: English edition. | Stanford, California : Stanford University Press, [2025] | Includes bibliographical references.
Identifiers: LCCN 2024049643 (print) | LCCN 2024049644 (ebook) | ISBN 9781503642485 (cloth) | ISBN 9781503642492 (paperback) | ISBN 9781503642508 (epub)
Subjects: LCSH: Voice (Philosophy)
Classification: LCC B105.V64 G86 2025 (print) | LCC B105.V64 (ebook) | DDC 128/.3—dc23/eng/20241121
LC record available at https://lccn.loc.gov/2024049643
LC ebook record available at https://lccn.loc.gov/2024049644

Cover design: Michele Wetherbee
Cover painting: Ricky Gumbrecht, *Yellow 2*, 48" x 24".

dedicated
to my daughter Laura Teresa
and to the beautiful volume of her voice

Contents

ONE   **The Knot of the Voice**   1
*Energies of Impulse and
Conceptual Intersections*

TWO   **Voices and Existential Spaces**   18
The Fabric of Everyday Worlds

THREE   **Singing Along**   41
The Emergence of Mystical Bodies

FOUR   **Voices in History**   63
Living Through Ontological Discontinuity

FIVE   **Voices and Imagining**   101
On the Verge of Agency

SIX   **Voices with Neutral Perfection**   127
The Address of Transcendental Authority

SEVEN   **Overwhelming Voices**   155
An Unconcealment of Closeness

Gratitude for Intellectual Closeness   183

Notes   187

Lives of the Voice

— ONE

The Knot of the Voice

ENERGIES OF IMPULSE AND
CONCEPTUAL INTERSECTIONS

WHEN I REMEMBER MY MOTHER who died in the summer of 2012, a few months short of her ninety-first birthday and wrapped in dementia, I can never hear her voice. I distinctly recollect her northwestern Westphalian accent that did not change at all during the seven decades she lived in phonetically different South Germany. This accent, her way of articulating, indeed became "my mother tongue," so much so that people who meet me today regularly and wrongly assume that I grew up in the northern part of the country. But the accent that I will use until I die at some point split off from the *sound* of my mother's voice, which I have irretrievably lost.

My father's voice, by contrast, is a burning presence with a somehow physical impact I am not able to escape. He was a remarkably handsome man—in the style, as some of his admirers said, of Hollywood actors from the 1940s, Clark Gable being a favorite comparison. He also achieved professional success and considerable wealth as a surgeon, at least until a certain point of his life, counting eminent national figures among his patients in the early Federal Republic. His voice, however, did not fit his looks, success, and status—at least not in his only son's perception. As I am writing these words,

I can hear his voice—a feminine tone but not in the high-pitched sense; it was more of an alto, similar to the voice of the less handsome and much more eminent Niklas Luhmann, a thinker who fascinated German intellectuals of my generation during the final decades of the past century.

Today, it is embarrassing to try to explain what irritated me so much about the voice of my much beloved father. From an early age, I became aware of an intense impulse to compensate for what I experienced as a fundamental weakness that his voice manifested. And I feared the signs and consequences that such weakness generated. Did my mother often seem attracted by other men—men with lesser looks, success, or wealth but deeper voices? Had I heard one such voice in our apartment one evening before I fell asleep, after eating scrambled eggs with a faint medicinal taste? Were there fewer of those famous patients who sometimes invited our family to lavish restaurant dinners and spectacular vacation places? When I was eight years old, my father and I spent a New Year's week as guests of a former National Socialist minister of the economy in a splendid villa on the Italian Riviera—where we were never invited again. And then there were those endless stressful discussions between my parents about the hospital's decision to scale back the number of beds in the department for which my father was responsible, a decision made after he had been absent from work for several extended periods due to illnesses that I could not detect. One summer my father and I, again without my mother, went on a vacation to Lake Constance, close to the Swiss border. During the long car ride, I actively kept our conversation as brief as possible because hearing his voice was so painful.

All those ways of coping with that impression of weakness have had a lasting effect on my life. After a difficult start in elementary school, I made every possible effort to pay close attention in class and invested endless hours in homework so that I could become a visibly outstanding student, a student with the highest grades in every subject, a student who never missed a single day of school until my graduation from gymnasium. I was even popular enough among my peers to get elected student body president. After all, the honor of the family was at stake, and I had to defend it every day, with the obvious result that I never enjoyed school. There was never a moment when such problems and my reactions to them detached themselves from my father's voice.

As I approached puberty, I anxiously worried about my changing voice, that it might change into my father's adult voice. This was a nightmare beyond my control, unlike my grades or popularity at school. So I started every morning with a self-imposed test—clearing my throat, speaking to myself, or singing—to try to figure out whether my new voice had finally emerged and what it sounded like. At some point, later than most of my peers, I recognized, to my tremendous relief, that my adult voice would be at least "average deep." And I was lucky indeed. My voice is between baritone and bass. It has turned out to be a voice that serves me well at academic and public events because its volume can fill large spaces without using a microphone. But while I still feel grateful, without knowing to whom, about this physical fact, I have never been proud of or even relaxed about my voice. Outside of everyday conversation, whenever I use my voice in public settings, I am still nervous about how it will sound, and then when reassured, strangely eager to show the world how strong it is.

Voices in general, not only my own, will forever be an obsession for me. I continue to measure strength against the perceived weakness of my father's voice, whose sound my imagination has kept acutely alive since his death in 2005. Quite literally, I am haunted by voices, and until recently I lacked the distance to think about them on a more abstract level.

In the present cultural and academic climate, an interpretation comes to mind, almost inevitably, that promises to resolve the traumatic impact of my father's voice. I have been the victim of a banal gender stereotype in assuming that my father, as a man, needed to have a deep voice and that the absence of such a voice exposed weakness that had a negative impact on the honor and standing of my family. It is no doubt true that men with an alto voice can be strong and successful in many ways, which implies that I should never have worried. And yet this retrospective commentary will neither undo the pain of my childhood years nor have a redemptive effect on the neurotic forms of behavior that it triggered.

So while my story illustrates a historical gender bias that we may hope to overcome, I can also see how it functions as an example for certain phenomena that are both essential in our lives and difficult to tackle. I will refer to these as belonging to an *ontology of individual existence*. What I have in mind are individual body features and how we perceive them in people with whom we interact. We certainly know that we cannot avoid reacting, in one way or the other, to tall bodies, to faces that we find attractive, to what we identify as physical deformities, or to the sounds of individual voices (we are supposed to remember and distinguish about a hundred such voices). At the same time, we have all learned that such spontaneous reactions should not play a role in our social behavior because they undermine a premise of equality that obliges us to ignore details that are not in the other person's control, like height, looks, or vocal quality. This is one reason we hardly ever deal with phenomena belonging to the ontology of individual existence. A second reason for the same abstention has to do with the fact that there are no rules for how we should process them. Faces that look attractive or voices that sound appealing to one person may have a repellent effect on another. Identifying shared filters of social knowledge that we all use in this existential dimension and that consistently shape our social relations seems impossible.

Among the phenomena pertaining to the ontology of individual existence, the voice is especially complicated. For one thing, in terms of meaning, the voice fulfills a double function. Together with writing, it is the medium through which we express propositional content that, broadly speaking, we have previously formed in our mind—and from this angle voices are different from body shapes, faces, or deformities, features that do not articulate well-circumscribed meanings. But at the same time—and in this sense converging with body shapes, faces, or deformities—voices trigger vague associations. One example is the embarrassing weakness that I "heard" in my father's voice whenever he was speaking. On this second level—and different from that of the voice as a medium for propositional content—it seems impossible to fully separate the associations triggered by certain physical features from those features that produce them. Here is one reason why I cannot think about my father's voice without hearing it in my memory.

At the same time, and also specific to the voice, it is impossible to fully detach the propositional content expressed by a voice from those subjective associations it also launches. When my father talked to me about the players from the 1954 world champion German soccer team I so admired, his voice continued to produce the embarrassing effect of weakness. This close, indeed inseparable, proximity among meanings, associations, and the physical perceptions on which the latter depend—what I call *the knot of the voice*—makes up the specific complexity of the voice as a phenomenon.

We process that "knot" whenever we listen to a voice in a language we understand, whereas we obviously miss the propositional content (meaning) articulated by voices in an unfamiliar language. Why certain voices remain in our memory with their sound (my father's voice) and others do not (my mother's voice) is another question with merely speculative answers. My imagination can, for example, distinctly produce the different sounds of my four children's voices. I also quite obsessively "hear" the voice of my great-grandmother Marie saying the same sentence—that she would "throw herself out of the window in front of the passing streetcar"—when living in a tiny apartment with the families of her sons became too much. Another voice that has stayed alive for me is that of her son Franz, my great-uncle, who in 1953 had returned to his hometown after eight years as a prisoner of war in a Siberian concentration camp. During our Sunday afternoon walks, he would suddenly call out in a deep, irritatingly melodious and nasal voice, "Free I want to be, free, free!" Then one winter's day he hung himself from a tree, and several weeks later his frozen body was found covered with snow.

I do not believe, however, that the permanence of certain voices in our memory is a result of dramatic or tragic circumstances. For example, the voices with which actors imbue the characters they embody may be random, but they often become an essential part of their engaging performance. I have always enjoyed how Marlon Brando, in the first part of *The Godfather* trilogy, gave Vito Corleone a perfect Italian American accent with an underlying tone of serious friendliness and even warmth that made me sympathize with the mobster. But while I could describe in great detail what I am hearing and the feelings that Brando's voice triggers in me, I would not be able to say why exactly it has that specific effect. As I remarked earlier, there are no socially objective codes that determine how we process the sounds of different voices.

Among phenomena making up the ontology of individual existence, voices thus seem to resist any conceptually systematic grasp. Even so, they have received considerable attention in the humanities during the past six decades. Based on a competent critical reading of Edmund Husserl's philosophy, voice became foundational within Deconstruction as the intellectual style inaugurated by Jacques Derrida's first book *Voice and Phenomena* from 1967.[1] According to Derrida, the fact, often highlighted by Husserl himself, that we listen to our own voice while we are speaking is responsible for the conviction that we are also able to understand, analyze, and describe our consciousness in its totality. Referring to the inevitably temporal structure of consciousness and language, Derrida wanted to expose this belief as an illusion: an illusion beginning with the discursive unfolding of Plato's philosophy in the form of dialogues—that is, with characters who listen to themselves while they are speaking—an illusion, finally and above all, that Derrida saw as foundational for the entire metaphysical tradition in Western thinking.

While it was not Derrida's intention to eliminate vocal phenomena from topics to be contemplated in the humanities, during the 1970s and 80s, the voice concept was viewed negatively and was temporarily excluded it from ongoing philosophical debates. Against this background, it is quite astonishing that the voice, more specifically the singing voice, had an almost ecstatic comeback in the late work of Friedrich Kittler, one of the founding figures of media studies—all the more so as Kittler was closely aligned with Derrida's philosophical positions. The first volume of Kittler's unfinished history *Music and Mathematics* highlights performances of ancient Greek rhapsodes as the "first victory of serene knowledge" because they allowed the singers and their audiences to capture and to ultimately describe in mathematical terms the prosodic structures to which they adhered.[2] Here Kittler saw an original connection between music and mathematics that media studies would further explore, the association having produced ever new developments and genres throughout the centuries.

Because Kittler, with remarkable mythographic talent, brought together conceptual configurations of his own time and dense images of what he viewed to have been decisive historical moments, the new academic discipline of media studies settled on the voice as one of its favorite topics. The German book *Stimme*, edited by Doris Kolesch and Sybille Krämer, is representative of several collections published in the early twenty-first century dedicated to the topic.[3] In the preface, and after explicitly distancing themselves from the topic's negative connotation coming from Deconstruction, Kolesch and Krämer outlined the book's two main goals. Given the fact that, by then, voice had already become the focus of many different academic pursuits, they first insisted on the need to work toward a new repertoire of specific concepts capable of overcoming the centrifugal diversity among different disciplinary traditions. Second, Kolesch and Krämer wanted to showcase the broad variety of historical contexts and cultural dimensions in which phenomena of voice were of central relevance.

Without a doubt, the twelve essays published in their volume provide a colorful impression of the topic's multiple fascinations from a high level of particular expertise. There are contributions about the history of opera voices and about voices produced without human bodies, through modern technology; there are essays about the power of voices in political rhetoric, about the functions of animal voices, and about silence in art, literature, theater, and ritual. What *Stimme* fails to achieve, however, is a philosophical basis for a new, integrated terminology or perhaps even a unifying theory. Are authors and editors to be blamed for this shortcoming or is it the inevitable result of the topic's specific internal complexity? Can we truly imagine concepts that comprehensively apply to the three different phenomenal layers that are simultaneously in play, and that need to be taken into account, when we speak about *the knot of the voice*: that is, voice as a medium of language (where the relation between the level of the signifier and that of the signified is "arbitrary" in the sense of Saussure); voice processed as part of and as a symptom of the speaking person's character or psyche (where the sound cannot be separated from the associations it produces); and voice in its pure material being (where scientific tools of description seem to be most appropriate)?

We may certainly dream of a utopian philosophical environment or of an individual philosophical genius capable of producing such overarching and yet coherent concepts, but against the background of our different discursive traditions, with their inherent limits and mutual tensions of incompatibility, it seems unrealistic to expect such a solution. This may explain why, during the past decade and behind the stereotypically repeated promise of stunning interdisciplinary plurality, the fascination of voice seems to have lost some of the energy that has permeated its remarkable academic history since 1967. Is it too late for a book on the "lives of the voice"?

One of the few intellectual impulses that encouraged me not to give up on such a project came from the true explosion of (not always fully developed) insights in Roland Barthes's famous essay "The Grain of the Voice," written in 1972.[4] Barthes had not offered any hints for a solution to the philosophical problem concerning an integrative terminology that Doris Kolesch's and Sybille Krämer's volume tackled without success a good thirty years later, but he moved in the direction of some difficult conceptual distinctions and incompatibilities that converged with intuitions about the knot of the voice. I also sensed in his text a contagious enthusiasm for some related aesthetic effects, for he dealt with voice from a perspective of singing, more precisely from the performance practice of the mainly German repertoire of *Kunstlieder* (art songs). Evoking songs as "the space where a language meets a voice," he called "the grain of the voice" those cases where the voice simultaneously functions "as language and music," as he progressively developed the "music" side in his essay.

Barthes's highlighted simultaneity of language and voice does, of course, occur not only in singing but in all situations where we use voices. The focus of singing as a primary example, however, makes more palpable the difference between voice as a medium of language and voice as a specific trace of the speakers' or the singers' individual bodies. Here probably lies the reason for the productivity of Barthes's approach.

From his initial notion of "the grain of the voice" as simultaneously language and music, Barthes proceeds to a distinction between two dimensions of singing that he refers to as "phéno-chant" and "géno-chant."[5] Phéno-chant includes

> all the features pertaining to the language sung . . . , in short to everything that serves the functions of communication, representation, expression, to what one normally talks about, to the tissue of cultural values.

Géno-chant, by contrast, corresponds to

> the volume of the singing or speaking voice, to the space where meanings [*significations*] sprout [*germent*] from the innermost language and from its very materiality; to a play of meaning [*jeu significant*] that is alien to communication, representation [of feelings], expression.

What matters the most here is the focus on the "sprouting" of a special type of meaning (previously called an "association") inherent to the "materiality" of language.

In order to illustrate the difference between phéno-chant and géno-chant, which occurs in every use of the human voice, Barthes refers to the performance styles embodied by two singers of *Kunstlieder*: the then-famous German baritone Dietrich Fischer-Dieskau and the Swiss baritone Charles Auguste Louis Panzéra, whose art Barthes had admired passionately for many years. Fischer-Dieskau appears as the champion of phéno-chant—that is, as the master of the "stupid organ [*sic!*]" of the lungs and of respiration, as the singer who maximally fulfilled "the clarity of meaning" ("la clarté du sens"). Panzéra, by contrast, stands for géno-chant, for the "metallic vibration" in both the vowels and consonants of the French language that he was producing:

> Panzéra pushed his "r-sounds" beyond the norms of the singer, without denying these norms: his "r's" were certainly rolling "r's," as in all classical art of singing, but this rolling had nothing of a peasant or of a French-Canadian accent: it was an artificial rolling, the paradoxical state of a sounding letter that was completely abstract (due to the metallic brevity of its vibration) and completely material (due to the moving throat as its obvious root).

Increasingly, the "tyranny of meaning," unilaterally attributed to Fischer-Dieskau, comes up short in Barthes's aesthetic estimation, which is quite plausible for an art form often confronting its listeners with languages they do not understand. What would be the point of reaching maximal transparency in a discourse inaccessible to most of them? But the bias against phéno-chant should not let us forget that in most everyday situations we simultaneously, inseparably, and yet differently react to both the meanings articulated and to the physical sounds brought forth in the utterance of a voice. Barthes, by contrast, leaves behind the side of language and finishes his essay with a thesis exclusive to the aesthetic function of the voice as purely material sound, a thesis quite typical for French thinkers of his generation:

> [T]he "grain" is the body in the voice that sings, in the hand that writes, in the limb that performs. If I perceive the "grain" in a music . . . , I need to establish a new, doubtlessly individual form of evaluation because I am decided to hear my relation to the body of the man or the woman who sings or plays, and this relation is erotic but by no means "subjective." (It is not the psychological "subject" in me who listens; instead of strengthening—or expressing—the relationship, the lust ["jouissance"] that the subject hopes for will rather undo it.) That evaluation has no law, it rejects the law of culture and of anti-culture.

I do not agree with the implicit assumption that every relationship mediated by the grain of the voice between different bodies needs to be "erotic" and lead to "jouissance" (a concept mostly associated with orgasm in French). Yet I retain Barthes's insight that the type of bodily contact emerging from the use of our voice is neither subject based nor conforming to any rule. No code made it necessary for me to sense weakness in my father's voice to which I was connected, nor was it my individual choice or interpretation to do so. Existentially, the fatherly voice has had a decisive impact on the course of my life, whereas epistemologically its status remains largely uncertain and thus an intellectual challenge.

Barthes conjures up the complexity and the not-only intellectual appeal of the knot of the voice through a double strategy whose two components collaborate without being discursively complementary. Daring to do so comprises the breakthrough quality of his reflection. Above all, he shows how—and in some cases why—concepts from the Western philosophical tradition never fully grasp the phenomena that he tries to pinpoint and paradoxically gets us closer to their understanding in the process. At the same time, he illustrates the topic by activating memories that his readers may have from the performance of singers like Fischer-Dieskau or Panzéra.

Such a double procedure seems to impose itself with practical necessity in any intellectual writing about the voice. As for the epistemological side, the situation is indeed even more complicated than what Barthes describes because, strictly speaking, the classical mind/body distinction both works and does not work for most cases concerning the knot of the voice. It does work for voice as a medium articulating propositional content, and it does not work for the other phenomenal layer that Barthes calls "the grain of the voice." It is precisely this state of fundamental ambiguity in the functioning of the available conceptual and discursive traditions that prevents us from dealing with the topic with a coherent argument—inductive or deductive—as my original book title, *Phenomenology of the Human Voice*, would have suggested.

A similar problem concerns the relationship between the phenomena of voice and the concept of presence, which has fascinated me throughout my career.[6] Quite obviously, presence in the sense of Latin *prae-esse* ("being in front of")—that is, presence as the spatial dimension that we cannot help developing between our bodies and other material objects in their environment—plays a crucial role within the knot of the voice. But there is no way of keeping "presence" neatly separate from the "sprouting of meaning" in a voice, as my typological distinction between "presence cultures" and "meaning cultures" tries to suggest. For, in returning to a previously discussed paradoxical formula, voice is, and is not, a presence phenomenon.

Such difficulties must have motivated my friend Eva Gilmer's soberly accurate remark that "voice" makes for a "disorderly topic," a topic, as we have said, that does not lend itself to an epistemologically coherent and discursively continuous exposition.[7] The problem, however, is not exclusive to the topic of voice or even to phenomena belonging to the ontology of individual existence. It seems to come up whenever we try to think or to write about human life without reducing the concept of life, as we normally do in the humanities, to its non-physical dimensions.[8] Seen from this angle, the multiple conceptual difficulties that I have been subsuming in the expression "the knot of the voice" turn from a reason to avoid confronting the topic in its full complexity into an impulse to embrace it. If we want to deal with phenomena of human life in a non-reductive way, then we need to accept and to cope with the epistemological difficulties as disorderly topics. The human voice is certainly not the only such case, but it may have a potentially paradigmatic status.

In the absence of a single solution that can claim to be phenomenologically and epistemologically necessary, what would be a good presentation structure for a comprehensive book on the human voice? As I tried to find a practical answer to this question, I remembered how, more than ten years ago, I was struggling with a similar problem in searching for the form for the book *Atmosphere, Mood, Stimmung*. That this happened in relation to a concept whose German word (*Stimm-ung*) has *Stimme* ("voice") as its root encouraged me to return to a solution I had used before. The most efficient strategy for the comprehensive presentation of disorderly topics may be to circumscribe them, in the almost literal sense of the verb. This means, on the one hand, that we leave empty the discursive space of the topic's systematically necessary but epistemologically impossible unfolding and, on the other hand, surround this conceptual void with a series of essays on partial aspects and the specific phenomena involved. Such delimiting presentations can never claim any degree of completion; they have no pertinent order or logical ending and tend, as we saw in Roland Barthes's essay "The Grain of the Voice," to rely on illustrating their topics with colorful individual examples. At the same time, the lack of a pertinent thematic structure allows for reading the different chapters of my book independently from each other, as long as there is space for the reminder and repetition of some basic conceptual premises.

What would be the intellectual—and perhaps even existential—point of trying to define the human voice? How is it different from the centrifugal plurality offered by multi-author volumes like Doris Kolesch's and Sybille Krämer's *Stimme*? I believe the act of demarcating voice and the process of understanding that it suggests align with how we live our lives—normally without thinking much about them. We live our lives by activating the capacities of our bodies and minds in a constant shifting between different existential dimensions—from sleeping and dreaming to eating, walking, driving, pursuing our professional work, speaking, listening to others, reading fiction, enjoying music or a landscape, having sex, shopping, thinking about investments, and sleeping again. These dimensions are always intertwined and overlapping, but we hardly ever go through them twice in the exact same order. Our existential everyday journeys thus produce intensity and boredom, density and exhaustion—without an essential core or a logically necessary ending. *Lives of the Voice* thus appears to be a suitable title for a book that follows such existential lines without any phenomenologically pertinent structure. The better I manage to show the different dimensions of the voice—juxtaposed, overlapping, intertwining—the more engaging this book should become.

The six following chapters cover a range of topics—from the different social effects of the voice, to an extended reflection about its possible status in historical time, to ways in which voices both permeate and transcend individual existence. In Chapter 2 we start with the question of whether there is a human equivalent to the habit of certain animals that mark their territory with the repeated production of sounds. From this perspective, the second chapter develops the highly flexible concept of existential spaces that go back to relations of distance and closeness between individual bodies and that are mainly regulated by the physical interventions of their voices. While these existential spaces, astonishingly perhaps, still seem to function as the primary fabric of everyday life in our electronic age, they have hardly ever reached states of habitualization or institutionalization, which makes it difficult to grasp their processes of emergence, transformation, and vanishing and may explain why, in spite of their ubiquity, we normally have but a vague awareness of them.

From existential spaces developed out of voice-based interactions as the fabric of everyday life, we proceed, in Chapter 3, to the impulse to "sing along" with other voices, which produces a specific type of community. Different from the knowledge-based social forms normally addressed in sociology, these social forms presuppose the availability of certain bodily functions and include bodies in their substantial presence (without implying any religious connotations, I am using the theological notion of "mystical bodies" for this particular way of being together). As a familiar paradigm for mystical bodies, we focus on the collective singing of stadium crowds. This approach requires, firstly, a proposal for the distinction between speaking voices and singing voices and then an analysis of a specific mode of atmospheric intensity, of some surprising effects (among them the capacity that the gospel refers to as "speaking in tongues"), and of some inevitable risks (above all, violence) set free by the function of voices in mystical bodies.

Rituals of singing along have occasionally prompted theories about a content-free processing of voices as the medium of prehistorical states of human sociability, and we take up this question in Chapter 4, which is dedicated to different layers in the relation between voices and time conceived of as history. More even than the foregoing discussions about voices and different types of sociability, their historicity unfolds a wide range of different ontological layers, conceptual discontinuities, and practical problems pertinent to our disorderly topic. To begin with, we of course have no documentary sources for voices from the times preceding the invention of sound recording shortly before 1900. But while this is emphatically true for the millennia in which the human voice must have developed into the medium for the articulation of meaning, we can look at mythological narratives that deal with this very emergence and its conditions. From the angle of its epistemological ambiguity, the voice turns into a test case for Hegel's view that body organs cannot belong to what he defines as the dimension of history because they do not mediate between the World Spirit and the spirit of human individuals. Ultimately—and rather than one central, overarching insight—our focus on the status of the human voice in historical time offers multiple illustrations and challenges to think through the existential consequences of its ontological and epistemological complexity.

In the final three chapters we deal with different instances in human existence where voice effects transcend the reach of individual control and agency. My father's voice became traumatic for me because I was unable to evade or at least to mitigate the unpleasant scenes it activated in my imagination. Chapter 5 returns to different aspects of the interplay between voices and imagination. That we above all and quite spontaneously associate hallucinations with voices demonstrates that they occupy a dominant status and authority in the dynamics of our spirit. To understand this seldom mentioned status, however, makes it necessary to develop a new concept of imagination that allows us to distinguish the specific impact of acoustic perceptions and their consequences on our mind.

Chapter 6 is about voices that some religious people believe are voices of transcendental beings. Rather than understanding voices as the product of the human imagination, the three classical monotheisms describe these phenomena as the voices of their gods. How do the different mythologies and theological traditions describe—or imagine—these voices and how do the voices relate to and interact with individual secular existence? Taking off from this question, we discover a surprising divergence. In Judaism the Torah conjures up God's voice in multiple forms and tonalities, with the point of convergence seemingly deriving from a desire to give contact with transcendence an ontologically impossible immediacy. In contrast, the Christian scriptures separate the voice of God from the sphere of incarnation and thereby from the life of Jesus. God and God's voice are remote, requiring that priests be delegated certain roles and functions. Islam, with yet another divergence, seems to have succeeded in establishing an unconditional authority for God without recourse to any concepts and images as anthropomorphic as the voice. A reflection on the familiar association of individual conscience as the highest level of an intrapsychic and therefore secular authority, with a (for most of us) strangely neutral voice, concludes the chapter's discussion of the voice's relation to levels of transcendence in the sense of ontological superiority.

The final chapter transitions to a quite different (in my case, mostly pleasant) sense of being overwhelmed by real (primarily recorded) individual voices that have been essential to me; quite literally, I cannot imagine my life without them. Since childhood (and probably due to the absence of classical opera in my education), five voices from popular music—Elvis Presley, Edith Piaf, Janis Joplin, Whitney Houston, and Adele—have given me the consoling and sometimes even ecstatic joy of a physical closeness that I experience as irresistible and yet outside any individual choice. Those voices *happen* to me, not unlike the figures of parents and siblings who determine our lives on a horizon transcending our will, which we call fate. Retrospectively, I believe that the voices of Elvis Presley, Edith Piaf, Janis Joplin, Whitney Houston, and Adele became crucial for me in moments of transition and provided an experience of substantial closeness that could not have emerged from personal encounters or conversations. Rather, they gave me the sense and even the certainty of a possibility to hold onto something that prevented me from getting lost and from vanishing in formless complexity.

Now while I don't intend to highlight such unpersonal closeness and the chance to hold onto it as a final thesis or as an existential dimension toward which this entire book and specifically its final chapter are heading, it condenses and makes concrete the possible yield that a confrontation with the disorderly topic of the voice from its different perspectives may provide. I think it corresponds to the sense of a contiguity "in the flesh" with other humans that permeates our individual existence—a contiguity and not a union in the flesh because we cannot abandon or transcend our own bodies as the condition of individual life. Nevertheless, a contiguity, more than just a shared condition, offers a spiritual connection with others that is constantly differentiated by and broken down into changing degrees of spatial closeness and distance that both connect us and separate us from them. This always present and never stable relation in space is the challenge that our voices process and absorb.

TWO

Voices and Existential Spaces

THE FABRIC OF EVERYDAY WORLDS

SOME FIFTEEN OR TWENTY YEARS ago, if I saw someone walking alone while speaking in a conversational tone, together with a register of lively facial expressions and bodily gestures, I might have believed that such a person was suffering from hallucinations. At that time, I did not yet have a place in my expectations for such behavior. With the frequency of their appearance steadily growing, however, even I, particularly naïve about what the then-emerging Silicon Valley industries had to offer, had to learn was that, instead of hallucinating, these individuals were involved in verbal exchanges with others who were absent in space. I had overlooked the hardly visible devices enabling them to listen to other people's voices and to transmit sounds of their own.

But, despite this realization, I am aware of a distinct absence in this behavior that I still have a hard time accepting. Although my mind can easily supplement images of bodies and reactions of other people whom the solitary speakers may be addressing, I miss the impression, if not the concrete perception, of a space that they jointly occupy that thus brings them together—and in which resides two or more voices in their different tonalities. Therefore, and despite my better knowledge, when I see someone walking alone and talking, it still looks like the symptom of a pathology to me.

When I try to articulate what I am missing in this scene, the first expression that comes to mind is a "social space." Then, however, I sense that these two words suggest a dimension and a degree of institutional stability that does not really belong to casual conversation. Examples of such established social spaces where voices are involved are parliaments with their protocols, classrooms and other settings for teaching at different levels of education, and gatherings for elaborate forms of religious services like the varieties of the Christian Mass. Those who act or function in such frames adopt a specific social knowledge containing choreographies for bodily movements, complementary expectations about the movements of other bodies, and also orientations for rhythms in the investment of voices. During my short spell as an altar boy in the still-Latin liturgy of the 1950s, I became aware that the functions of voices were largely exempt from articulating any meaning in this context. By responding to the priest's two words "Dominus vobiscum" with the four words "Et cum spiritu tuo," we inevitably created a stable, dependable, and also somehow visible social space, although the content of these words was not at all clear to us. "Rituals," as we can call most social spaces in the proper sense, quite regularly subordinate the meaning they produce to mostly implicit rules for bodily movements.

Casual conversations, by contrast, seem to be less separated from meaning and less rule bound. They may fulfill certain locally and historically specific standards of politeness, and they may observe certain hierarchies of rank, but we are normally not capable, as with social spaces in the form of rituals, to predict how they will develop or under which conditions they may come to an end. They are highly individual indeed on quite a number of levels—individual, as I just said, due to the openness of their different trajectories and endings; individual because of the mostly non-synchronized expectations and impulses of those who perform them; individual because, when people talk to each other frequently, they do not necessarily take into account the form of each previous conversation; individual, finally, due to the physical difference in tone and volume between the voices used, a difference that tends to get bracketed and even neutralized within rituals and their stable social spaces. Later I will try to demonstrate that the physical quality of the voices produced in existential spaces plays a largely underestimated, and indeed a crucial role, in our individual existence.

These are some of the reasons why I propose to refer to the spaces that emerge from and accompany the more casual variety of verbal interactions as *existential spaces,* based on our use of the word "existence" in association with general features of human life as individual life. The astonishing diversity of existential spaces explains why, on the one hand, they are almost ubiquitous while, on the other hand and due to their individuality, they tenaciously resist description by abstract concepts. What further contributes to their elusiveness is their ongoing alternation between expansion and contraction. To pinpoint existential spaces as "phenomena" almost seems to contradict the ancient Greek meaning of the word (as things that "show themselves") because existential spaces do not show themselves as stable forms, despite being so constantly audible—and visible—to us that we interpret their absence as a pathology. Given, however, their true ubiquity and the importance that voices have for existential spaces, I believe their interplay deserves the unavoidably precarious attempt of a patient and detailed analysis. We start out with five descriptive perspectives and dimensions.

One of the more remarkable aphorisms in Ludwig Wittgenstein's *Philosophical Investigations* urges a shift in the way we use the concept of understanding to help us gain perspective on the process by which existential spaces emerge: "To understand a sentence rather has an affinity with the understanding of a musical motif." Wittgenstein wants his readers to approach understanding in an existential space as one would a piece of music. With music, we do not care about possible meanings or about the intentions of the composer or those who perform. Rather than focusing on propositional content and the intensions of the speakers articulating that content, Wittgenstein suggests that we react to the sound of voices as we do to a musical motif: by adjusting our bodies in relation to the sound waves produced. Depending primarily on their volume, we want to be closer to or further away from sounds and their sources; we may adjust the position of our ears to the direction from which the sounds are coming; and we may seek a body position in which we feel comfortable or sufficiently attentive. With all these body movements, we inevitably create and transform the spaces we are part of.

Simultaneously, we allow musical motifs or the sounds of individual voices to trigger moods and images in our minds that we feel somehow correspond to the acoustic impressions. But while moods and images are inseparable from existential spaces in their always changing objectivity, whether or not such impressions of a correspondence exist between them and different sound sequences cannot be answered as we cannot be inside any other person's mind or psyche. This impossibility, however, does not prevent moods and images from being a vital dimension in our understanding of voices or musical motifs. Generally speaking, and with sound waves produced by voices being time phenomena only existing in constant change, understanding them happens through the process of constantly readjusting our body positions, images, and moods to them. So closely are the sounds of music and of voices indeed connected to these reactions that when we speak of a "melody," we refer more to what they evoke in our psyche than to a layer of their physical objectivity.

Returning from musical performance and Wittgenstein's provocative aphorism about understanding a sentence like a musical motif to conversations and their voices, and shifting from the emergence of existential spaces to their structure, we can see how, as a second feature, an elementary, mutual, and twofold asymmetry dominates in them. By "asymmetry" I want to highlight the fact that, within existential spaces, we primarily concentrate on the other person's voice while we barely perceive our own voice in the background (which is not to be confused with the condition that, due to effects of human anatomy, we hear our own voice differently from the way that other people hear it). The asymmetry is twofold because, exclusively concentrated on the other voice, we can only modify our own voice depending on what we perceive. As an effect of these two levels of asymmetry, the paths that the mutual relations in sound and emotion between two voices may take are under nobody's full control and therefore unpredictable: each voice reacts, without coordination, only to its speaker's perception of the other voice.

The unpredictability of a trajectory evolving from the interaction between two voices is even clearer than the paths of content emerging between two speakers because we have much more flexibility and differentiation in adapting to the meanings produced by other speakers than in responding to them on the sound level. Thus the trajectory of the interplay between two voices may sometimes sound raw and uncultivated, like processes observed in nature before we begin to sense possible regularities that determine them. Rather than belonging to our agency, their elementary objectivity appears random. Singing voices, by contrast, do not normally conform to this dynamic emerging from the mutual structure of double asymmetry. For singing voices tend to become independent elements within interactions and thus cancel out the precarious and unpredictable relationship between two speaking voices. This may account for the impression of artificiality, mostly on the stage, that duets often evoke. For while the singers and composers may think of them as a musical representation of everyday conversation, duets require a degree of deliberate coordination from another perspective that everyday conversations, due to their objective randomness, neither require nor achieve.

From the emergence of existential spaces and from their internal structures we now turn to their plasticity, as a positive counterpart and different perspective on unpredictability and randomness. In our everyday life, we are able to distinguish, remember, and recognize as many as a hundred individual voices, and we also know that no two voices are perfectly alike in their physical qualities (above all, in volume, tone, and in what Roland Barthes called "the grain of the voice"). This is why, unlike with singing voices, we hardly ever try to categorize speaking voices. As a result, the relations between each two different voices and the existential spaces that they produce in their interactions have to be unique, including the expansions and contractions that the existential spaces are going through. This also applies to each time that we restart interactions between voices because they are only minimally shaped (if at all) by the trajectories of previous interactions. But what we may thus call their high degree of plasticity does not correspond to a similarly high level of flexibility in their adaptation to the different situations where they occur. Rather we see a large horizon of diverse possibilities, mainly depending on the physical qualities of the voices interacting. In this sense, voices and their existential spaces constitute an odd dimension within historical and cultural worlds. They provide these spaces with an important, perhaps with the quantitatively most important, layer of physical substance, but they hardly become part of their institutional forms.

As a fourth effect of existential spaces, we have already mentioned how voices trigger those individual psychic states that we call mood or atmosphere. Interestingly, *Stimme*, as the root of the equivalent German word *Stimmung*, assigns to voices an emblematic status in triggering moods—although moods can also be reactions to multiple other modalities coming from the surrounding physical world and hitting the surface of our bodies, among them quite obviously music, but also light, temperature, or weather.[1] Meanings articulated by voices only play a subordinate role in this process. Nobody has yet been able to fully describe and explain how different types of physical touch determine moods as different states of the mind, a process for which Toni Morrison invented the beautifully compact and paradoxical formula of "a feeling like being touched from inside."

Moods or *Stimmungen* thus constitute yet another layer of existential space that evades human agency and meaning. We all know from personal experience how an individual voice that we find unpleasant is capable of casting a dark shadow over the content of a message that we would otherwise enjoy. Even more complicated is the relation between *Stimmungen* provoked by different voices and our imagination. Different from the connection between mood and meaning, we probably feel less of a tension or of a convergence between mood and imagination, but rather feel the effects of specific colorations with which different moods permeate images or other intentional objects in our consciousness triggered by perceptions. From this perspective, we again arrive at those unanswerable questions about individual states of mind and their potential consensus within existential spaces. Can something like joint, synthetic mood effects emerge from the interaction between different individual voices? Will multivocal conversations as comprehensive units move us to overarching *Stimmungen* or do the different voices of which they consist prevail as separated acoustic triggers of psychic effects?

What we call intonation, as a fifth layer of existential space, seems to get us closer to social conventions than the emergence, the effects, the plasticity, and the mood-triggering functions of voices, without being fully controlled by the objectivity of their structures. Linguistic theory gives intonation the status of a "suprasegmental phenomenon": that is, of a comprehensive tonal sequence that can modify the understanding of the meaning produced by a sequence of words. The functions of different speech acts—for example, congratulations, prohibitions, or love declarations—are often secured or differentiated by such intonational patterns. We normally do not have to deliberately choose the appropriate intonation to convey a meaning, but, on the other hand, we are not always sure we have appropriately perceived the intended functions in the intonation of other voices.

Irony, a quality of speech that gives a sequence of words a meaning opposite to what they explicitly articulate, often results in uncertainty. My wife, who thinks of me as irony-resistant, regularly overemphasizes her ironic intonations in our conversations. Yet, I have to admit that, after more than thirty years of marriage, I am never quite certain whether I am reacting the way she expects and wants me to. If even an individual voice cannot be certain of controlling different intonations, how can we make any assessment about a sequence of voices and interactions? And are intonations contagious? Do specific individual intonations—such as warnings, insistences, or affirmations—prompt a reciprocal intonation in a speech partner? Are we likely to speak ironically when we are exposed to an ironic intonation? Do intonations with opposite effects cancel each other out in a conversation?

Our process of going through five different dimensions and perspectives of existential spaces and of the voices from which they emerge has established a recurring sequence of observations. Each time we start out with phenomena and mechanisms familiar to all of us from our everyday lives, and then we advance to questions about the interactions between them that inevitably lead to zones of uncertainty and endless individual differentiation, zones where general concepts no longer apply. This confirms the specific position that existential spaces and voices occupy in societies. While voices do make up a large portion of social interaction, only a comparatively small part of this vocal substance belongs to the dimension of social conventions or receives the focus of our individual attention. Voices and existential spaces are an essential dimension of our lives, but it is a dimension that essentially belongs in the background, individually and socially. Therefore, whenever we turn to this background substance of our existence, we perceive sounds and sound movements that lack apparent regularity and therefore resist our efforts to identify any general features in them. If voice is a disorderly topic, existential spaces comprise a disorderly part of reality.

But there is more to existential spaces and voices than just a resistance to conceptual and theoretical description. Due to their status as a background substance, they permeate our lives with multiple effects that we barely notice and whose origin we ignore. I believe that Paul Celan's poem "Stimmen" ("Voices") from the 1959 collection *Sprachgitter* (*Speech Grille*) deals with voices from exactly this perspective.[2] It starts out, as the title "Stimmen" announces, from a premise of plurality, and instead of unwrapping the phenomenon with stable concepts, images, and potential moments of experience in a line of argument, the poem approaches voices in a circle of specific instances that leaves open a space for individual associations and feelings.

In addition, the sustained underlining for the word "Stimmen" in each stanza can suggest an impression of materiality far from the meaning-conveying function of voices. One instance that surrounds the topic refers to the background status of voices in relation to the meaning that they articulate:

Stimmen, nachtdurchwachsen, Stränge
an die du die Glocke hängst.
Wölbe dich, Welt:
Wenn die Totenmuschel heranschwimmt,
will es hier läuten.

> Voices, night-knotted, ropes
> on which you hang your bell.
> Dome yourself over, world:
> when death's shell washes up on shore,
> a bell will want to ring.

Voices are a part of the material three-dimensional "world that domes itself over" and that thus become a background upon which hangs the bell from whence meanings will ring. As part of the world's material substance, voices blur the individuality of human emotions and push them back into different stages of nature, from the mother's heart to the process of growing trees:

> Stimmen, vor denen dein Herz
> ins Herz deiner Mutter zurückweicht.
> Stimmen vom Galgenbaum her,
> wo Spätholz und Frühholz die Ringe
> tauschen und tauschen.

> Voices that make your heart
> recoil into your mother's.
> Voices from the hanging tree
> where old growth and young growth
> exchange rings.

Being nature, voices are also infinite, but it is not an infinity ("*Unendliches*") like that of the human mind or the human psyche; rather, voices are a never-ending flow of "[herz]schleimiges Rinnsal" ("runnels of [heart-]slime"). Are they slime because they can never be rid of the materiality from which they emerge? This what the word "*kehlig*" ("guttural") in the poem seems to propose:

> Stimmen, kehlig, im Grus
> darin auch Unendliches schaufelt,
> [herz-]
> schleimiges Rinnsal.

> Voices, guttural, amid the debris,
> where infinity shovels,

runnels of
[heart-]slime.

From the first stanza, where voices appear as events and thus produce discontinuity in human observation—"Stimmen ins Grün / der Wasserfläche geritzt. / Wenn der Eisvogel taucht, / sirrt die Sekunde" / "Voices, scored into / the waters' green. / When the kingfisher dives / the split-second whirs"—the poem circles around, with its images and scenes becoming more distant from the meanings that voices produce with each rotation. Finally, they turn into "late noise, stranger by the hour" ("Spätgeräusch, stundenfrei"), a "gift" to thought that thought cannot process, also a noise that refuses to stop being part of life, like a scratched leaf refusing to wither: "ein / Fruchtblatt, augengroß, tief / geritzt; es / harzt, will nicht / vernarben" ("a / carpel, large as an eye, and deeply / scored: bleeds / sap, and won't heal over").

As they move away from meaning, voices become nothing but matter in Celan's poem—matter detached from humans and their minds, but matter, that by refusing to heal over or to stop bleeding, also returns to life. Thus voices become purely physical life in the end—"no voice" ("keine Stimme") indeed, as Celan's last stanza states, physical life in its own infinity and abandoning all emotional individualism, physical life perhaps that, transformed from a medium of articulation into an existential space as matter, energizes human existence "as a gift," as something that we no longer discard.

Going back to our description of the voice as a knot of human life—in which meaning, imagination, moods, and sound are intertwined—we could then say, inspired by Celan, that voices in existential spaces are sound, mood, and imagination, with meaning moved to the periphery. It is of course impossible to ever completely bracket and isolate meaning when we listen to a voice, as the impulse to interpret words will always be part of our existence—or push imagination as formless substance of content towards a limit where it turns into a fully meaningful structure. But with meaning at a distance in existential spaces, we can see how voices as a background with their interactions and interferences turn into the main matter and fabric of our everyday lives. They become a fabric of life in the sense of a material texture without which, as its substance, social life does not exist, a fabric, finally, in the sense of a background for whose internal forms we have little attention and hardly any concepts.

Once we have identified existential spaces with their voices as a fabric of life, once we have understood that their background status is both a condition and a consequence of their function as substance, and once we have also realized that being substance and background exempts them from standard ways of understanding, how can we go any further in capturing their functions? To find a solution, I will use the traditional phenomenological distinction between experience (*Erfahrung*) and lived experience (*Erleben*). "Experience" refers to the process by which physical perception becomes an intentional object in our minds and finds a meaning by the application of an element of social knowledge that we have stored. In the case of "lived experience," by contrast, we do not employ elements of social knowledge for the intentional object in question. This is the case—and the problem—with many aspects of existential spaces and their voices as the background substance of our social life. Because we cannot transform these phenomena into experience, we try to evoke their effects under the subjective perspectives from which we encounter them in our lives—that is, we to try to evoke them as lived experience. To clarify, I will discuss the effects of existential spaces and voices on three different levels: under which conditions we feel good about them; through several mini-narratives concerning processes of change and how they relate to existential spaces; and with a practical distinction among the types and functions of existential spaces and their voices.

When do we feel good about existential spaces as the constantly changing, non-institutionalized substance of our interactions? The first mildly paradoxical answer to this question is we feel good about them as long as we don't notice them. Not unlike organs of our bodies that only become objects of attention when their functions stall and pain gives them the status of intentional objects, interactions and existential spaces that we do not have to think about seem to flow in a natural and pleasant way. Once we notice, however, that the person we are in contact with is trying to modify the course of the interaction, we either react negatively or may even abandon the relationship. Why would we want to be in a non-goal-oriented process if that process requires effortful correction and change? This is a reaction different from more formal social spaces where initiatives to modify structures based on consensus between the participants occur quite frequently, with the intention of preserving or maximizing their functions.

The positive tone that we often sense in existential spaces and their voices resembles the vibrations of a well-running engine. We don't need to do anything about them, and we don't worry about how they will perform in the immediate future. Quite frequently, such impressions of a pleasant flow are the effect of voices producing a rhythm that brings them together without interventions of intentionality. We call "rhythm" any practical solution for the problem of how time objects—for example, interactions between voices—can adopt a form. The very problem between time objects and forms has to do with the elementary contrast in that the former (time objects) are in constant change whereas we consider the latter (forms) to be stable relationships between phenomena and their environments.

How can the interactions between different voices, as time objects, then assume a form? It happens as soon as we have the expectation (or even ambition) that their relation shall be *productive,* in the sense of bringing to the fore new states of quality or new movements that did not belong to these voices before their interaction began. The alternative to such productive relations is interactions that, in their ongoing exchange, regularly return to sequences of modifications that they have already gone through before. If this happens—in an interaction between voices, for example—repetition substitutes form as a non-moving stability that time objects in themselves cannot maintain. Nothing else substitutes for the principle of rhythm.

But rhythms not only remove potential worries about the productive development of interactions: they also lower the tension of mind or consciousness among those involved. Such lowered tension between people using their voices along rhythmic patterns seems to allow imagination to occupy the foreground of concept-based thinking with its high tension of mind, a shift that further grounds affinity between existential spaces as a fabric of life and imagination as non-conceptual layer of mind. Much more than formal social spaces and practical efforts of thinking, existential spaces thus become a source of imagination—and also of moods. From the opposite perspective, side, rhythms and their flows of imagination will never emerge as long as we try to provoke or even create them.

And how do we live through the mostly precarious continuity and through the never- ending changes of existential spaces? As I said before, this continuity often means reiteration. Every weekday morning, I arrive at Coupa Café in front of Stanford Library at around 7:30, which normally makes me the first customer, and I then always order a large cappuccino and several cans of mineral water. Only a small number of employees are working there so early, and with each of them I share a recurring pattern in the exchange of voices and intonations. We make our words sound friendly, and the range of variation is small. A specific emphasis in our expressions—an unexpectedly gloomy or jubilant ring, or an answer different from the usual "good" to the unavoidable question "How are you?"—would obligate us to produce non-functional speech acts for which we have neither content nor time. So we always keep the same distance across the counter of Coupa Café, exhibit the same smiles, and after the short waiting time, I take my cappuccino and the five cans of mineral water to the table where I always sit. On the rare days when one of the employees volunteers to bring the coffee or the water to my table, we go through a short moment of imbalance in our relationship, due to the extension of our usual existential space—an imbalance that requires apologies or gestures of particular gratitude on my part in order to return to our protocol and to its routine that we enjoy. Finding our way back to reiteration provides a good start to the day.

About nine hours later and after a walk of some twenty-five minutes, I arrive home to a different elementary exchange of voices, an exchange with a much greater emotional charge and a broader range of variations. For while I mostly enjoy the daily work of reading, thinking, and above all writing, I also spend my library office afternoons with a longing for my wife's presence that constantly grows. So shortly before seven, I open the house door by turning the key in the lock to the left (a mechanical mistake) and loudly say "Good evening, darling," wanting to sound like a loving husband (neither a variation there nor a completely relaxed routine). I speak rather loudly indeed because I do not know whether she is at home and, if so, in which room—closer to the front door or further away—she will be working, reading, or watching TV in that moment. No response means she is not there—but it may also mean (fortunately a rare occurrence) that her silence is a sign of irritation.

On a normal evening, however, the tone of Ricky's response, more than its specific words, functions like the key in a musical piece. She surely does not deliberately choose the tone of her voice each time. But every weekday evening, the first relation between our two voices quite literally sets the tone for the next hours of serious, casual, gossipy, or loving conversation; the tone for dinner at home or in a nearby restaurant; and often also for a walk around the neighborhood. No doubt the tones—or the "keys"—that emerge also depend on memories of the day, on specific plans for the evening, and on moods (or mood swings) of which we are partly aware, or not. But, above all, an unpredictable layer and background effect comes out of the relation between our voices each day and from the specific existential space they produce, with its higher or lower intensity. If sometimes there are "keys" that we don't enjoy or find to be inappropriate for the course of the evening, we may want to modify them, although this requires words that may turn out awkward, even between us. One way or the other, good key or bad key, the moment of coming home is a voice moment with a decisive impact on the end of the day.

Individual voices not only change in mostly unpredictable ways in different situations, but they also produce stories according to age. Especially in male adolescents, we expect a transition in the voice of a child to the deeper and more voluminous voice of an adult. During this transitional period, there is an odd oscillation between different tones as the adolescent speaks (German has the rather dramatic word *Stimmbruch*, "breaking of the voice," for the process). Parents, siblings, teachers, and friends customarily expect this period to be synchronized with a move toward adulthood, often to a degree that overestimates the actual emotional and intellectual transformation that is taking place. When I first heard the new voice of my fourteen-year-old grandson Diego, I was surprised to see that he was still approaching me as he had since he was a toddler, with the same tender hug and the same kisses on my cheek. Diego, probably due to an insecurity that is typical for his stage of life, was clearly hoping for continuity both in the physical and in the emotional ways of our relation, and yet something objective had changed between us. With the new relation between his young voice and my old male voice, our existential space had assumed a different substance giving an unfamiliar flavor to our words and feelings. It was an objective new reality, a new substance that we embodied. To some degree, we will never be able to capture, let alone control, this new existential space in its impact on the ways we love each other.

An age-bound voice transition in the opposite tonal direction has impressed and quite surprised me during the past years. Due to a chronic disease, one of my lifelong friends and most admired colleagues lost his baritone voice that used to be part of his particularly appealing physical presence—a loss indeed, more than a change, because there is hardly any volume now left in his whispering articulation. It has turned into a whisper. As Justin had forgotten to warn me, we passed some difficult minutes during a first encounter after several years, due to my incapacity to hide surprise and also embarrassment about the need to get closer to him in order to understand what he was saying. Once he had used the standard diagnostic words to describe his situation and assured me that he had found new forms of behavior to compensate, we quite deliberately started to develop new body gestures, vocal volumes, and rhythms for our existential space. Today I can say that our friendship has certainly not suffered—although it has changed. It changed not only because Justin's serenity and composure have increased my admiration, but because I cannot help showing this increased admiration and my unnecessary eagerness to lend support, and because it turns out to be difficult for me to forget Justin's no longer existing voice. Above all and similar to the effect of my grandson Diego's voice change, the background substance of our existential space is no longer the same. A whispering voice does not make my "heart recoil into another heart," it will not turn into "[heart-]slime" nor into "late noise / stranger to the hour"—to use some more of Celan's poem. On the other hand, Justin and I sense that the change has been intellectually productive for us. Both gain and loss have given the continuity of our friendship a new existential space—and a new liveliness.

A different loss occurs whenever one of the speaking voices in a conversation turns to laughing or crying. Such events normally bring the ongoing vocal interaction to an end because only an immediate turn of the other voice to laughing or crying can be a substantially adequate reaction. The continued use of words and syntax or silence on one side, by contrast, interrupts the exchange. Laughter that is not spontaneous invariably sounds unnatural and awkward, and the emergence of tears is under nobody's control, whereas words in response to tears or laughter assign the speaker the rather undesirable roles of a therapist or a commentator. Sudden tears or laughter thus either deeply transform existential spaces by provoking mimetic reactions or, in most cases, make them collapse—leaving open the option of starting them over again after a reasonable amount of time.

Sometimes voices change in ways that are not age-related, and their existential spaces can be described as a crescendo that has no tonal objectivity. For more than a year, I met every Thursday morning with Andrea, an advanced doctoral student, at the same Coupa Café and the same table where I drink my daily cappuccino. With unusually sustained concentration, we focused on the projects and written versions of his dissertation chapters whose outstanding quality prevented us from getting lost in the most recent items of local university small talk. I had a moment of discontinuity on the day that I noticed, while mentally replaying some of our recent conversations and their arguments, how I was able to physically imagine Andrea's voice with its distinct tone and rhythm—to a degree that suggested I was able to copy it. This realization seemed to have an impact on the form of our exchange. At least a part of our existential space's background substance had now become an intentional object for me. I liked the sound of Andrea's voice, I was looking forward to its live perception each time that we met, and I observed how I was involuntarily modifying the volume, the tone, and the pace of my own voice to an extent that sometimes gave our vocal interplay recognizable forms. While I could not say that the content and the style of our conversation was changing, I realized that a friendship had begun to grow when Ricky and I first invited Andrea and his girlfriend for dinner—a friendship that has survived Emily's and Andrea's departure to the East Coast. No doubt my new perception of Andrea's voice in my head had triggered this crescendo—without being its reason. I now often hear his voice in my mind, and, by associative inversion, it makes me remember Andrea's dissertation chapters and imagine his next book project.

What exactly determines the voices that I can actively remember and those that I cannot? Decisive, for me at least, seems to be the quasi-acoustic impression that certain voices leave (but can memories really have a sound?), an impression that, at a younger age, used to be connected to the temptation and capacity to copy them (I have meanwhile lost this competence). Other voices, as I already said, I am able to describe in detail—without hearing them. I have no confident answer to this question. My father's voice I still hear because it so embarrassed me. Andrea's voice, by contrast, I simply like and want to hear again. Ricky's voice sounds almost too close to be an intentional object for me—rather, it is the physical core of my life that assigns to other voices their places.

The greatest number of voices that my memory can recall somewhat precisely are the warm voices of men who protected and supported me during my years as a student and a young academic: the caring voice of Kilian Volk, my teacher during my second year of elementary school; the voice of Joseph Fick, my most admired high school teacher who sounded like someone speaking German with an American accent; the correctly Bavarian-sounding voice (an oxymoron somehow) of Karl Riedl who, as a high-ranking state administrator and director of a distinguished fellowship group, presided over our lunches in Munich after 1967 and gave me the idea of spending a year at Salamanca; the clear (I almost want to say "transparent") voice of Harald Weinrich, a renowned Romanist of the postwar generation, who read some of my early academic essays without any institutional obligation and gave me serene encouragement; and the surprisingly melodic voice of erudite Karl Maurer, a senior colleague at the University of Bochum, to whom I owe my first tenured appointment.

Why most of the voices that I can physically remember are male voices I do not know. Could it have to do with my persistent impulse to copy them? That so many of them belonged to men who supported my educational and professional progress most likely leads back to an enduring insecurity and lack of confidence, with its desperate need for emotional substance—and thus has much to do with the ways these voices sounded.

Finally, what I have been saying about the reasons for almost physically recalling some individual voices strangely does not apply to memories of media-transmitted voices, to voices with whose owners I never shared an existential space. Unlike the voice of my mother, I do distinctly hear the singing voice of Edith Piaf, like a gift from the depths of time, with a force that absorbs my attention and isolates me from the present.

I have developed some distinctions between types of existential spaces, mainly depending on their different inscriptions into time, on a level of lived experience. The first type of existential space is quite ephemeral and brings me back to my daily walks to work. As I am leaving home at an early hour, I only see a few people coming from the opposite direction, which may explain why on most days I like making contact with them (or is it just Californian friendliness?). Early morning runners are excluded, as obliging them to utter words would interrupt the rhythm of their breathing. To those, however, who use a non-athletic pace, I say "hello" or "good morning" and feel delight whenever I hear their voices respond (which does not always happen), letting an existential space emerge between us that lasts just for the few seconds of seeing each other and vanishes in the moment that we are mutually out of sight. While I hardly ever try to imagine where the other person is going or what may be the reason for her getting up as early as I do, the mini-event of our short-lived existential space gives me jolts of energy. Reactions from others I encounter that do not involve sounds do not have the same effect on me. And, those whom I see regularly and therefore expect are becoming part of a more habitual and less energizing layer of my everyday.

By temporal contrast, academic seminars—in particular seminars on the graduate level, with between five and fifteen students sitting around a table—have often fascinated me as a slow-motion process of existential spaces emerging from voice interactions and turning into more formal social spaces within the protocols of the academic institution. Where participants choose to sit and how their voices sound are not normally the focus of the instructor's attention during a first meeting. She will concentrate on the propositional content of the students' contributions and on the level of knowledge, argumentation, and motivation that they exhibit, allowing for an initial judgment on how the class may evolve and on whether it will be possible to reach the set intellectual goals. From the second session on, however, students approximately repeat their seating arrangements and adjust their voices accordingly. They seem to be increasingly comfortable with these patterns and therefore do not think, let alone speak, about the topic. With a few exceptions, it remains impossible to extrapolate the reasons behind such patterns of body distribution in a seminar, but they often end up turning into soundscapes whose contours resemble the deliberate form of a choir. We thus witness the paradox of an informal existential space producing the effect of an established social space.

During my final teaching seminar at Stanford in the winter of 2018, I felt at times like I was playing the role of a conductor. To the right, at the far end of our joint space, I had come to expect the voice of a young woman who liked to speak early on, often immediately right after my introductory words, with an intonation of passionate conviction; during the final minutes of the sessions, the more skeptical sounds of a male voice quite regularly came from the opposite left side. Closer to me and in the middle was a group of voices prone to fast-paced exchanges, and halfway to the back, I could see the sometimes-lively reactions of participants who never turned into speaking faces. As different individual students and groups noticed, I began to expect their voices from certain places at certain moments of our seminar sessions and was increasingly adapting my own interventions to this sequence. Probably I should not push any further the metaphors of choir and conductor, whose connotations of formality and intention are ultimately inadequate to the fluidity of existential spaces. But whenever participants remind me of how that Stanford seminar reached an enjoyable intellectual intensity, an intensity whose individual voices we vividly remember, I trust that the slowly emerging substance and form of its soundscape worked as a condition of success. At the same time, I do not fully understand, let alone assess, the relation between this type of an internal existential space and the effects that it is producing. Without being spiritual, existential spaces can enhance intellectual life.

Decades ago, when the intellectual stock value of Freud- or Lacan-inspired concepts and arguments was much higher than today, it would have felt compulsory and even exciting to point to the erotic underpinnings of teaching situations. While this observation has long since turned into a truism (which the ruling political correctness does not tire of condemning), it may yet appear all too farfetched to approach erotic situations—inside or outside educational settings—from the perspective of voice investment. For if we can say that in educational frameworks different voices have a chance of developing specific soundscapes in a sustained process, the intensity of erotic encounters tends to make voices vanish. Words and voices do have their obvious functions, however, in the stages of foreplay. There are libraries of canonized texts describing strategies or behaviors through which speaking will both secure and intensify what present-day English language calls erotic chemistry. A reliable next step to get erotically charged existential spaces closer to sexual interaction is "talking dirty."

In the process, the volume of voices, the temporal extension of their use, and the explicit content they carry are fast receding indeed, up to a point where their remaining presence becomes the anticipation of an imminent absence of physical sound. With this transition existential spaces implode. Erotic mastery has often been identified with the capacity of giving maximum time to this stage between a minimum of voice investment—and silence. For when voices turn frail and finally disappear under the impact of overwhelming body stimulation, an exclusively physical interaction with its precarious temporal synchronization begins. The control effects of thought and agency are ceasing, and two (or more) bodies transform from being an existential space into being one physical substance. Between them, quite literally, there is no distance left to be mediated by voices.

Now while we normally associate the return of voices in erotic situations with the peak moment of orgasm, a less eroticized commentary may interpret this comeback as the reemergence of communication and of existential spaces. A faster breathing rhythm that produces non-articulated vocal sounds functions as a message of precarious bodily synchronization, a message about the imminent ending of a bodily process in its stage of irreversibility. We want to reach this stage of irreversibility, and then both desire and fear to arrive at its ending. This willful abandonment of agency has been decisive for the position and value of erotic situations in most human cultures. Voices with their vanishing and reemerging existential spaces indeed surround the expanse where two irreversible and non-synchronized bodily processes happen—and in the luckiest case join each other. Voices lead into and out of this stage. What qualifies them to do so are the layers of physical touch, of imagination, and of moods in the knot of the voice, with meaning at a distance. Voices are both within and outside agency; they are the medium enabling us to fulfill the intention of losing agency.

Phone sex, without the possibility of turning into existential spaces, can help us understand the specificities and the limits of vocal behavior in erotic encounters. Quite obviously voices fulfill a dominant if not an exclusive function here in the foreplay stages that mutually produce growing excitement. But in the case of telephone sex, the moments of their fading cannot announce and anticipate the silence of purely physical, irreversible, and never fully synchronized bodily processes. On the contrary, silence in phone sex marks an entry into the solitude of self-stimulation. Stated differently, it does not arrive at the threshold of willfully abandoning agency, at the threshold where existential space is vanishing and being replaced by one state emerging out of the convergence between two bodies. From an ontological standpoint, we realize that technically mediated voice interactions may project a glimpse, an impression, and even an illusion of space but definitely not a space in which bodies can physically relate to each other under conditions of distance, proximity, and touch—a space where they can shake hands, exchange material objects, smell each other, or have sex. This of course also applies to more advanced—that is, to more sensorially sophisticated media facilities, like Skype or Zoom. They all fail to provide a physical space where bodies have the possibility of relating to each other without voice mediation.

At the core of media-based relations, voices are reduced to become an unfulfilled promise of existential spaces or, if we want to emphasize that technologically mediated voice exchanges do have a (limited) physical impact on their participants, they reach a status of "second order existential spaces." As such, technically mediated voices tend to activate a focus on the meanings articulated by voices that is much more concentrated than under the conditions of bodily co-presence. For the substance or fabric of life in the background of existential spaces is ontologically separated and not available to these voices, and they thus miss those dimensions that control their human agency. Precisely this condition causes the distinct feeling of a lack, of something missing, when I see solitary walkers talking to others who aren't present: they have abandoned or have simply lost the fabric of life.

For all the temptations and even merits of phone sex, what dominates technical media in general is this impulse to return to and stay with meaning. Its strength also pushes back and dries out the fluidity of imagination a state of mind not permeated and structured by concepts with their distinctions. Although it would seem natural that our minds immediately produce images of faces and bodies for the voices that we hear and are talking to, our mental behavior in technically mediated conversations instead seems to resemble that of communication through a written or printed text. For it can only take into account language. We thus understand why the modalities of remote teaching that we all have gotten used to during the pandemic years were so very efficient from the perspective of knowledge transmission. Remote teaching does not even require the traditional rituals and formal conditions of teaching situations that were meant to isolate students and teachers from potential distractions. Distance learning—and distance life—clearly have their advantages.

But what do we lose if, by using technical media of communication, we increasingly abandon existential spaces and thus isolate voices from their bodies and from the fabric of life? Above all we lose access to world and life as spheres of reality that are not fully dominated by mind, meaning, and agency. This includes a sense of the world as material plurality, plasticity, and variation that functions as a way of maintaining and intensifying sensorial relations to our environment. With voices separated from their spaces thus becoming the object of an exclusive focus on meaning, we also weaken imagination and moods as products of the mind that are triggered by the impact of the material world on our bodies—and therefore stay remote from deduction, induction, and argument as operations of the mind. Without voices in their existential proximity, above all, we will lose a pleasure in and about our lives, whose beauty used to depend on never becoming an object of exclusively conceptual attention.

THREE

Singing Along

THE EMERGENCE OF MYSTICAL BODIES

FOR MORE THAN HALF A CENTURY, the city of Rio de Janeiro took pride in possessing the largest stadium on earth—and arguably in human history—with the only plausible competition being the ancient Roman Circus Maximus, about whose capacity opinions diverge. Constructed for the 1950 Soccer World Cup tournament, exclusively adapted to the spatial rules of this sport, and today surrounded by one of the city's few neighborhoods without any special appeal in its landscape, architecture, or history, the big Rio stadium bears the popular name "Maracanã" (from a nearby river). Originally it offered space for 200,000 spectators, and thus used to reinforce Brazil's South American reputation of a society prone to megalomania. The Maracanã gained its aura by association with Brazil's rise and status, during the second half of the twentieth century, as the world's leading soccer nation. This rise began, traumatically and by counterpoint, with a defeat at the hands of neighboring Uruguay in the 1950 World Cup final, and it was reinforced by Brazil winning five world titles with charismatic national teams with legendary players like Pelé, Garrincha, Zico, and Romário. They all considered the Maracanã and its crowds to be the central stage for their athletic art.

When the World Cup came back to Brazil in 2014, there was no doubt that it also had to return to this stadium, after a necessary structural and functional overhaul that downsized its capacity to around 80,000 spectators. As I happened to teach a seminar at the Pontifícia Universidade Católica in Rio during the week of matches celebrating the Maracanã reopening, I convinced my wife and our daughter, who had traveled with me, that the stadium deserved their visit and bought tickets for a game between Flamengo and Vasco, two of the most renowned local franchises. The price of the tickets seemed to assure a safe location with good visibility. I was thus quite appalled when, arriving a good half hour before kick-off, I realized that our tickets seated us in the center of the famously loud, hard-core, fierce, and simply dangerous Flamengo fans. This crowd is called, with more than a slight fascist connotation, "a Falange," and its members were already chanting their hymns in the usual aggressive spirit and with a comprehensive spectrum of pornographic words. I was relieved to think that Ricky and Laura, with only peripheral knowledge of Portuguese, would at least not understand these lyrics and wanted to suggest that we quickly buy seats elsewhere. But, to my amazement, I saw that they had joined the Falange fans in their rhythmic jumping and were singing along with them in what sounded to me like a remarkably smooth Rio accent. Never before in my life had an act of singing along impressed me so intensely—and so emblematically.

A sociological perspective, light years away from the emotions triggered by our Maracanã experience, would of course suggest that the voices of the Flamengo supporters were key for their specific reality as a social body and that, by singing along, my wife and my daughter had quickly become part of it. On this most general level of observation, singing and singing along do indeed converge with the constitution of existential spaces through voices in everyday conversations. But it is even more obvious that the structural elements and the effects of singing along, not only in a stadium and with hard-core fans, differ on many levels from those of casual or serious speaking between individuals in their everyday interactions. Anticipating this contrast with existential spaces, I will try to unfold concepts for a description of several dimensions that make up the act of singing along.

I start with a proposal for the distinction between singing voices and speaking voices. From there we move on to elaborate the difference between joining, with a singing voice, social bodies that already exist and perform in a space (like the Flamengo crowd that we encountered at Maracanã) and, on the other hand, the plasticity that characterizes the ongoing co-production of existential spaces. Next we focus on the mainly, but not exclusively, physical conditions that arise in the impulse to sing along (among them the "gooseflesh" reactions often provoked by the perception of singing voices). As a central part of the conceptual work to be done in this chapter, we then analyze the specific appeal, intensity, and strength of the sociability that emerges from singing along in a crowd and that makes up one variety of what I call mystical bodies. The concluding pages, by contrast, deal with another type of mystical bodies corresponding to singing along with individual voices. All these considerations are presupposing the multi-dimensional topology of the knot of the voice as a frame of orientation and reference.

Although from early childhood we can distinguish between acts of speaking and acts of singing, it is difficult to come up with philosophically adequate concepts for this contrast. Helplessly inadequate metonymic or metaphoric approaches dominate among the rare attempts to do so (for example, the characterization of singing voices as "sounding like musical instruments"), and musicologists have sometimes complained about this situation, without suggesting viable alternatives. I think we will more successfully tackle this task by beginning with a concentration on the different functions of singing and speaking voices than by collecting observations about their physical substance and form, as most proposals for a distinction have done in the past.

Speaking predominantly articulates meanings formed in the mind, whereas singing mainly exhibits our voices in their physical qualities, which does of course not preclude the possibility of conveying or receiving meanings at the same time. This is how we are able and often willing to listen for hours to singing voices in languages that we do not understand, while our attention to speaking voices ceases as soon as we realize that we are not familiar with the language they are using. Even in the performance of songs whose lyrics reach high levels literary quality (the most obvious historical genre being the German *Kunstlieder*), semantics never overshadow the sound of a particular voice for the listeners' appreciation.

But why does singing almost always depend on language, independently of the singer's literary ambition and level, if it is not really about content? How is singing typically an act, as Roland Barthes wrote, where "a voice meets a language"? To be sure, there is no unconditional need of words, sentences, or language in order to sing. We can make our voices be heard without borrowing elements from language, and we do so with utterances that listeners, used as they are to the voices' connection with language and its abstract categories, tend to identify as sequences of vowels.

Coming back, however, to the observation that voices are, philosophically speaking, time objects in the proper sense—that is, phenomena that can only exist in temporal extension—it appears convenient for their display, even in singing as a sheer showing of vocal qualities, to have available to memory previously existing forms along which they can unfold. Words, as sequences of vowels and consonants, make up the elementary level of such forms, independently of their meaning. Compared to vowels alone and due to their consonants, they have the additional advantage of bringing out acoustic properties related to voices that we would otherwise not notice, for example the rolling r-sound in Charles Panzéra's singing of which Roland Barthes was so fond.

Based on our previous discussion of rhythm as an overarching concept for how time objects can have a form, we also understand why words used for singing are normally assembled in rhythmic patterns. Rhythms not only constitute a more complex and extended form for the exhibition of voices than words alone, but they, due to the inherent principle of repetition, also make their respective forms predictable for the singer and expectable for the listener. As I mentioned before, rhythms come with the additional effects of coordinating bodies, of supporting memory, and of conjuring up, in seeming three-dimensional concreteness, textual objects of reference. Thanks to their rhythms, singing voices adopt these three functions as side effects that hardly ever belong to the singers' intentions. Finally, and following from rhythm as a form of repetition, singing voices often project themselves into stanzas, that is into the second level of repetition and variation of internally complex forms of repetition. By doing so, I believe, they suggest that, due to its structure, the performance of an individual song will arrive at an ending that, in the case of speaking voices, is an exclusively content-based intuition. Although no absolute limit for the number of stanzas can ever exist (I once listened to the live rendition of a small country's full national anthem in thirty-seven stanzas), it thus seems safe to assume that, as with form repetition, rhythm contributes to shaping the individual forms of singing events and to their listeners' expectations.

Above all, however, we associate singing voices with melodies—with manifold combinations of rhythm and pitch. Melodies activate a much broader variety of high tones and low tones than do speaking voices (thus exhibiting a wider spectrum of their physical qualities), and the occurrence of such varieties follows the specific structure of repetition inherent to the rhythm chosen. In their synchronized temporal unfolding, both as pitch and as rhythm, we hear melodies as entities that, throughout their variations, we can identify in vocal (but also in instrumental) music. Melodies are thus a further, particularly complex level of form for singing voices, the one level of form obviously that they do not share with speaking voices. And singing cannot happen without melodies, nor melodies without rhythm: melodies are the dimension of form that ultimately makes rhythm necessary for singing.

Together, all these form-related distinctions explain why it surprises and indeed often irritates us when we perceive a sustained melody with its rhythm in a political speech or in an academic lecture. Politicians and academics intuitively try to avoid the impression of singing because it would signal that, compared to the physical quality of the voices displayed, their thoughts are secondary or even unimportant to the ongoing communication. But how shall we then understand that, as the great Egyptologist Jan Assmann once pointed out, priests in different religions quite regularly transition from speaking to singing when their voices are supposed to occupy the place of God's voice (as occurs, for example, in the Catholic High Mass)? If it is correct to say that with such a shift the listeners' attention moves from a concentration on propositional content to a focus on the actual physical quality of the voice and on the body of which it is a part, we may speculate that in such moments of transition the main relevance of the situation goes from the meaning of God's revelation to God's real presence among humans—that is, to an ontological possibility explicitly implied in the theologies of all religions that cultivate and take literally concepts of incarnation. Singing voices thus transcend being a trace and a reality of other humans' presence in the spatial and palpable sense of the word; they also stand for the presence of transcendental beings.

Speakers in everyday conversations normally do not notice the first sound of spoken voices as an incisive threshold or discontinuity because voices have a clearly instrumental and thus subordinated status in such contexts. Whoever is involved in a conversation may remember the particular motivations and opportunities initiating the exchange or the plasticity in the development of their positions, arguments, and existential spaces, but the sound of the voices is not of major concern. For nonprofessional singers at least, the impulse toward singing hardly ever comes from "inside" in the sense that they have an individual reason to exhibit their voices in an otherwise silent environment.

Rather, singing typically presupposes the perception of an ongoing musical sound—vocal, instrumental, or mixed (including the memory of musical performance). In other words, we normally begin to sing under the circumstances of *singing along*, meaning that we have encountered an individual body or a group of bodies in the process of producing music with their voices or with instruments. Such preexisting music can also emerge from a media device, such as a radio, a record player, or a mobile phone. In such cases we do not literally share a space with the bodies of singers or musicians. They are spatially and often also temporally remote and certainly do not hear us, although we usually act in singing along as if they did. I will come back to this act of singing along with recorded voices, including the voices of dead people.

The normal situation that triggers singing along as an exhibition of voices converges with our experience in Maracanã. We were inadvertently faced with a social body that was comprised of the collective use of voices. The form of such jointly singing bodies can be described as a ritual, in the sense of a shared, informal, and mostly intuitive knowledge about the spatial distribution of participating individual bodies: to produce a sound together, they should, for example, neither stand too close to nor too far away from each other. There is typically no sense of the size or of the limits of such collective bodies, as they can grow or decrease inside a certain range, without immediately collapsing or abandoning their sound production.

The difference between what we call a choir and a singing body like the Falange of Flamengo at Maracanã is but a difference in degree. Choirs, too, have the status of rituals, but their underlying knowledge about spatial distribution reaches a much higher level of formality and differentiation. Positions of individual bodies in the collective body of a choir depend on the range and the strength of their voices because they are supposed to facilitate a specific sound effect that the conductor is aiming at and to which each voice makes a specific contribution. Choirs as rituals therefore come with an awareness of size, of limits, and of closure, an awareness that makes it less likely for spontaneous reactions of singing along among those who listen to them.

Music in general, as the German phenomenologist Helmuth Plessner described in great conceptual detail, presupposes and often activates a disposition of the human body to follow its forms. We sometimes repress this energy in our self-reflexive relation to our own body (for which Plessner uses the complex German notion *Leib*), for example, when we listen to an orchestra or to a choir in a concert situation. Among the reactions of our bodies to music, singing along is specific in two ways. First, while we cannot say that all body movements triggered by music structurally correspond to the musical sounds, singing along, in the first place and always, occurs as mimetic behavior in the full sense of the term. Once we release our control, the perception of singing voices activates our own voices, which spontaneously—and without any deliberate variations—try to be in harmony with the voices heard. Second, while instrumental music may inspire individuals to come together as collective bodies through dancing, the performing musicians will not be dancing. This is in contrast to voices, which can trigger listeners to sing also, joining the preexisting social body.

Altogether, it seems plausible to assume that vocal music, by provoking mimetic behavior on different levels, has a more elementary and thus a stronger impulse toward sociability than instrumental music. Roland Barthes went so far to say that informal singing along, different from singing in a choir, happens with the accepted risk or even the desire to "lose oneself" in the other voices, and he interpreted this inclination as an effect of our erotic drives. But, as I noted earlier, erotic drives may be less ubiquitous in human existence than Barthes's generation of French thinkers liked to assume. Whenever I watch and listen to the video of Whitney Houston performing "I Will Always Love You" from her and Kevin Costner's 1992 film *The Bodyguard*, I feel an impulse to join this stunning female voice with my less than mediocre masculine voice—an impulse indeed to really lose my own voice in hers, perhaps even to lose my entire existence for several minutes in the existence of somebody who died more than a decade ago. As this is all about becoming one with other voices and other bodies, their images and sounds hardly ever assume the shapes of objects that are independent from us—as would be the case in a situation of erotic attraction. Singing along works as an energy toward sociability more than toward object-specific desire.

Several times already I have referred to the "impulse" that prompts us to sing along, assuming that a particular combination of bodily and psychic movements exists that both reacts to the perception of singing voices and initiates the active use of our own voices in a mimetic fashion. For a closer look, we can distinguish between general, in this case largely empirical, knowledge about the impact of music on human bodies or on human emotions, and, more specifically, hardly ever empirical observations about functions connected to voices in musical performance. In doing so we return to the different dimensions of what we have described as the knot of the voice.

Without any expertise regarding the intersection between biochemistry and psychology, I will just point to four different hormones and their effects on our feelings that appear in most surveys about the impact of music on the human psyche. Listening to music releases endorphins that inhibit feelings of physical pain and at the same time trigger euphoria as an all-embracing openness to the world. Music also intensifies the production of cortisol and the related effects of healing that converge with the tamping down of pain thanks to endorphins. Likewise, it activates dopamine—the hormone of pleasure, satisfaction, and motivation—together with oxytocin and its capacity for erotic stimulation. While we take it for granted that exposure to music can make us feel upbeat and conjures up positive feelings on many levels, it is worth underlining that, from a scientific angle, such complex happiness does not remain locked in the sphere of an individual life but implies, through oxytocin, that there is a component that makes the closeness of other bodies attractive to us. Any type of music thus has a vector toward sociability that is independent of our volition.

What we call gooseflesh or goose bumps is both the visible and internally perceived bodily symptom of such hormonal releases. While we lack reliable research about differences between vocal and instrumental music in their impact on the biochemical level of human life, we seem to associate gooseflesh more with the perception of singing voices than with listening to instrumental music. Above all, we identify goose bumps mere seconds before we experience the often literally irresistible impulse that makes us start singing along. Once we are in the process of singing, the visible manifestations of our stimulated bodily excitement disappear and leave us with a less acute sense of communal happiness. Without referring to music and singing, Helmuth Plessner analyzes a structurally similar initial stage for the functioning of human voices in *Laughing and Crying: A Study on the Limits of Human Behavior*.[1] Like listening to singing voices, seeing and hearing other people laughing or, even more so, crying, can provoke goose bumps and, at the same time, mimetic reactions, although the possible reasons for laughing and crying do not converge with the impulses toward singing along.

According to Plessner, laughing and crying draw their energy from an incompatibility between different meanings, expectations, or obligations that simultaneously present themselves to us (we laugh if we can manage to live with such potential tensions and we cry if an impossible choice between such options is imposed upon us). Also different from singing, laughing and crying do not typically exhibit rhythmic forms nor are they connected to circumscribed meanings. Plessner therefore interprets laughing and crying as symptoms of situations whose challenges transcend the human capacities of sense making and thus interfere with reflexive control over our bodily impulses. Once the non-controlled body takes over, we laugh or cry.

As mimetic behavior, the tendencies to laugh or to cry with others suggest that abandoning reflexive control turns into a contagious impulse. In a similar way, we can speculate that the moment when we feel the impulse to sing along, often the goose bump moment, is when we let go and allow spontaneous mimetic bodily behavior to occupy the place of reflection, volition, and sense making. This impulse, which is due to an exceptional charge of positive emotional intensity triggered by the music, does not work in laughing and crying, because the challenges of an actual experience exceed the capacities of our practical reason.

Unlike laughing and crying, singing voices normally articulate meanings, meanings that mostly remain at the periphery of our attention. And this of course also happens on an objective level if the singers cannot understand the language being used (they still feel a remote instinct to interpret the words they hear). Does such attention to meaning, however peripheral—which sets singing apart from laughing, crying, and also from instrumental music—play a role in our fascination with musical voices? Seen from this angle, I find it astonishing how many successful songs, not only in popular music, produce meanings and trigger moods that we characterize as bittersweet. At first glance, bittersweet meanings and moods seem to be in tension with the overwhelmingly positive feelings that music generally produces (mainly, as we have seen, through the activation of a cluster of hormones). To invoke just two prominent examples of the bittersweet quality in popular songs: the lyrics of both Whitney Houston's "I Will Always Love You" and Adele's "Someone Like You" passionately and regretfully speak of loves that could not last. Songs with more neutral lyrics are the exception.

Of all philosophers, Friedrich Nietzsche, in fragments from 1871 regarding the chorus in ancient Greek tragedies, provides us with a way to understand such bittersweetness as a symptom of the complex impulse to sing along.[2] Nietzsche speaks about the *Tonuntergrund* ("tonal grounding") in any spoken use of the human language and distinguishes it from the *Geberdensymbolik* ("gestural symbolic") of the speaker, a concept that comprehends all phenomena that contribute to the production of meaning. The tonal grounding, by contrast, does not carry any meaning or content, although, the meaning is there from the initial moment when a voice begins to sound, in the tone of the speaker. Instrumental music, by contrast, cannot have tonal grounding in the full sense of this observation because it lacks meaning as a contrast.

Nietzsche goes further in analyzing tonal grounding by connecting it to the concept of the will (*Wille*), which, at this early stage of his thinking, was still close to the use that Schopenhauer had given it as a source of energy underlying all change and unrest in human life. But while Schopenhauer wanted to understand music in general as an "expression" of the will, Nietzsche repeatedly insists on its exclusive relation to the human mouth—that is, to the tone of any utterance produced by our voices (although he does not explicitly use the word "voice"). Further, and most importantly, he interprets the will in its relation to the tonal grounding as an elementary dimension (*Sphaere*) where, different from language in its function of the gestural symbolic, pleasure and displeasure (*Lust und Unlust*) are not separate: experience is more elementary or even profound than the dimensions of distinction and meaning production.

If tonal grounding is there from the first instant of any vocal uttering and if, in addition, we can say that singing specifically, different from speaking, assigns an only secondary status to meaning, then we can extrapolate that the will as a meaning-canceling non-distinction between pleasure and displeasure accompanies our acts of singing performance. Singing thus appears to be a case, perhaps the most elementary case, of what Nietzsche describes as the intertwinedness between tonal grounding and the will. As he states that the "the will underlies our entire corporality in the same way that the tonal ground underlies the word constituted by consonants and sounds," we may conclude that singing dissolves the always-tense relationships between the will and bodies controlled by reason and between tonal grounding and words controlled by meaning production. It may thus set free energies that have to remain contained as long as our mind centrally focuses on the production and communication of content.

If breakthrough moments for the purely physical body occur in singing, this can also explain why lyrics attached to songs tend to show semantic instabilities no longer structured by the type of distinctions that constitute similar meanings. Bittersweetness is a case in point—that is, as a layer of ambiguity based on the tendency of song lyrics to foreground elements excluded by homogeneous meanings. Nietzsche himself found "marginal" and "inadequate" the "ambition of lyrics" to give "images" or concepts to music and to the singing voice because he believed in a basic incompatibility between music and meaning. But this by no means contradicts the possibility that singing can have a destabilizing effect on the semantics articulated by lyrical texts.

Analyzing the impact of singing has shown us yet another configuration in which the dimensions making up the knot of the voice are converging and interacting. We like to expose our bodies to the sheer physical impact of singing voices for, as music, they produce intense and complex states of happiness without reflection. At the same time, we give in to the temptation to abandon the mind's control over our bodies and let well circumscribed meanings collapse into a floating instability of content. The voice thus again cuts through the field between physical and mind-based dimensions of our existence, the field that we call life, without having a concept to mediate between its ontologically different dimensions. Also belonging to the dynamics of life, the impulse to sing along initiates processes of emergence for a specific kind of sociability.

We have seen in the previous chapter how speaking voices contribute to the production of existential spaces for conversations in their endless plasticity. The tonal grounding, however, remains in the background of the speakers' awareness. For while we may describe their sound as the normally overlooked fabric of everyday life, voices and the bodies to which they belong don't typically play a role in the sociability of a business negotiation, an academic debate, or the casual exchange of memories among friends. Singing along, by contrast, is not only a process triggered by the internally complex impulse deriving from our contact with a collective or with an individual, but it also facilitates the emergence and growth of social forms that we cannot imagine without the inclusion of other people.

As sociologists have long prioritized definitions of society based on shared knowledge bases and paid astonishingly little attention to other forms of humans being together, I will try to elaborate on concepts for understanding the social structures and body presence that are involved in the processes of singing along. To set such social forms apart, I come back to the idea of the "mystical body" that has been used since the third century to describe Christianity as a not-only spiritual collective, based on the belief in God's incarnation and in his lasting physical presence among humans. My main example for the emergence of such mystical bodies in secular life is the act of singing along in a stadium crowd.

In what exact way did my wife and daughter become part of the singing Flamengo crowd at Maracanã? The Falange and also fans of the opposing Vasco were already there as visible groups when we entered the half-filled stadium, and most arriving spectators quite spontaneously headed toward their respective territories. Such movements can be seen as part of the "swarming effect" that joins all living beings, from bacteria to humans, as they gather around other bodies (not necessarily of the same species) with the double instinct of seeking closeness and avoiding collision. Among mammals, a stationary moment in which all individuals are using their voices in a roughly coordinated fashion often precedes collective movements, which may indicate a spatial intelligence beyond individual awareness and intention. Voices thus belong to the forces toward sociability—both on the most elementary level and on the highest level of behavior.

As the Flamengo supporters were not only physically present but already in the process of singing, they gave us an impression of euphoria and of abandoning bodily control and meaning formation. Among people sitting or standing next to one another in stadiums, a further (lateral) condition becomes relevant for the ongoing process of singing along, a condition that gives a more precise meaning to the concepts of "pure body reactions" and "purely mimetic behavior" used on the previous pages. Inadvertently and often without noticing, we copy all kinds of bodily movements that persons next to us—above all, persons with whom we do not communicate—are performing. This copying mechanism in the literal sense goes back to the so-called mirror neurons discovered a good twenty years ago. On the one hand, mirror neurons register movements of living beings near to us (again, not necessarily beings within the same species) while on the other hand simultaneously triggering analogous movements in the bodies that perceive them. Singing thus not only goes back to an impulse toward the convergence of preconscious psychic reactions, but it also presupposes and includes a dimension of pure bodily mechanisms. As we will discuss, this dimension has a particular importance for the tonal quality of individual voices within the act of singing along.

Based on the initial stage of swarming behavior and on the effects of mirror neurons, voices become the most important medium for the emergence of collective bodies that include individual bodies in their physicality. There are other conditions that consolidate the reality of mystical bodies and our respective awareness. People singing along in a stadium of course hear the sounds that their voices are producing together, and this feedback strengthens their internal coherence as collective bodies. But they also jointly concentrate on the scenes of the game as it develops, with movements of individual players unleashing the onset of copying movements in the bodies of many spectators. We feel the hint of an innervation in our arms when we see how the quarterback of the team we are rooting for throws a pass to his favorite receiver. This effect of transitive attention converges with lateral reactions from those around us, in a feeling of elevation that adds to the euphoria coming from the self-perception of collective voices.

Mystical bodies emerging from the process of singing along are therefore typically permeated by a particular degree of happiness, of a happiness sometimes verging on "ecstasis" in the sense of making individuals within a group feel "outside" and even "beyond" their everyday moods and capacities. The word most frequently used to characterize such individual states is "intensity," and I will try to give it an interpretation in relation to singing along and to mystical bodies. Singing along happens and mystical bodies articulate themselves in forms of rhythm—that is, in forms of ongoing repetition. Beside the functions of body coordination, of memory support, and of conjuring up imaginations on a high level of quasi-palpable concreteness, rhythms have an impact on our individual psyches—more precisely, on the tension of our mind (*Bewusstseinsspannung*), a phenomenon that we are familiar with but do not control. Being under the impact of a rhythmic sound or being part of a collective body moved by rhythm will always lower this mental tension. We are less focused in our individual attention, less oriented toward personal goals or motivations, and tend to let go—with mostly happy feelings.

Seen from this perspective, we can say that, mainly due to rhythm, when we join in a process of singing along, we subjectively experience mystical bodies in a way that corresponds to the initial stage of what Gilles Deleuze called "a body without organs."[3] A body without organs presupposes a previous situation where individual members of a group sense that their mutual relations are contingent, that is, they are open to many possible forms of connection. We have indeed seen how the impulse towards singing along happens as an urge of letting loose, and we can now add that we normally don't have an awareness of the swarming and copying instincts working somewhat contradictorily in the opposite shaping of collective bodies. In this sense, I was convinced that my wife and daughter would want to leave, and then I realized that they were singing along with the Flamengo fans and did not at all want to quit the group.

Intensity, according to Deleuze, is precisely the process leading from individual impressions of contingency to that of necessity, from absolute entropy to absolute negentropy, a process within which we sense that we can no longer choose our movements and are increasingly determined by the movements of the mystical body to which we belong. There is a remarkable discrepancy here. While "objectively"—that is, from the angle of the mystical body—our singing is formed from the moment we start singing along, we subjectively believe that we can quit or at least use our voice in the form of a variation. Only through spurts of intensity that occur in singing along do we subjectively begin to realize how we have become part of a mystical body—and we are normally enthusiastic about it. Once this has happened, we tend to participate endlessly, often up to a state of exhaustion. This process of intensity, which leads from an initial discrepancy between the objective function of anonymous form mechanisms and our subjective impression of contingency to their powerful convergence, seems to be a general feature of mystical bodies, not only of mystical bodies emerging from singing along. Historical evidence is provided by the infamous dance marathons of the 1920s that sometimes brought their participants to a state of deadly exhaustion.

None of the conceptual proposals elaborated so far—neither the distinction between singing and speaking voices, nor the analysis of the impulse that makes us sing along, nor the description of mystical bodies emerging from it—explains how we often manage in singing along to articulate with perfect, close to native pronunciation words, sentences, and texts in languages with which we are not familiar. The smooth Rio de Janeiro accent in the voices of my wife and daughter was the greatest surprise of our Maracanã adventure. I am equally stunned each time I attend a game of Borussia Dortmund, my favorite German soccer team, and hear almost 30,000 hard-core fans perform, louder than the stadium's sound system and with an enviably British accent, "You'll Never Walk Alone," the hymn adopted from Liverpool FC, although most of them have likely never taken an English class. This astonishing capacity is by no means exclusive to large crowds at sports events. My teenage grandchildren's foreign languages sound the best when they sing along with recent hits from popular music, and many opera singers, who give a marvelous Italian tone to arias from the classical repertoire, betray their native tongue when they converse in the same language.

It seems that we cease to struggle with the phonetics of foreign languages as soon as we stop using our voice as a medium for the articulation of meaning. My wife and daughter were clueless about the content of the words they were singing with the Flamengo fans. My grandchildren would rather associate the English lyrics of their favorite hits with their moods, for which they have no words, than with specific meanings. And opera singers care infinitely more about the quality of their voices than about the drama unfolded by the libretto. When we have distance from meanings, the sounds and the cadences of our own languages for everyday communication likely are not invoked and thus don't interfere with our pronunciation, as is quite regularly the case in pragmatic situations when we order dinner, make a political statement, or dare to tell a joke in a foreign language. Due to the absence of habitualized linguistic behavior, where the voice is always a tool of the content to be articulated, mirror neurons can take over the function of being the dominant impulse for sound production. They copy, through our voices, what we physically hear, simultaneously in our own singing—and independently of any meaning. Other factors may play a role here—for example, the wish for a harmony between the voices heard and our own. But above all our pronunciation in foreign and unknown languages gets better to the degree that it remains distant from thoughts, intentions, and meanings.

Singing along to the sound of individual voices feels different from becoming part of a collective body that sings. As I have mentioned, there are a number of voices in popular music, mainly voices from the past, that never fail to inspire me to join them. Except for one Adele concert in California that I attended from the cheap seat section I was able to buy during the first minutes of an electronic ticket sale, I have only heard my most beloved voices in recordings. I cannot say, however, that I experience this mediated distance as a shortcoming, for the physical impact of recorded voices on our bodies is hardly different from that of voices in the present (not to mention the technical devices that bring recorded voices into maximum physical closeness). My favorite popular voices and songs invariably give me the gooseflesh feeling although I have heard them hundreds of times.

My initial response—an impulse to sing along—is similar to the one triggered by a singing crowd, maybe even stronger. A first contrast seems to come from the fact that, unlike the voices of collective bodies, individual voices normally show a gender inflection. But while there may be more women than men among my favorite singers, I cannot discover a clear preference for one group or the other when it comes to my wish to join in with my own voice. The tonal distance that separates most women's voices from mine will never prevent me from singing along. Contrary to an initial suspicion, gender is not an important dimension for reactions to individual singing voices.

Does my reaction (wanting to sing along) depend on whether I see images of Edith Piaf, Elvis Presley, and Whitney Houston performing the song? I have already said that I find Whitney Houston to be exceptionally beautiful in her concert recordings and movies. But my reaction is still the same if, for experimental reasons, I close my eyes while I sing "I Will Always Love You" to the sound of her voice. An easy way of describing this impression would be to say that the type of mystical body that emerges from the process of singing along with an individual voice exclusively consists of the two voices involved. The listener's simultaneous activities of hearing and of singing, however, do produce a structural asymmetry between his voice and the voice that he copies because the voice that he copies is not accompanied by self-observation, whereas all participants in a collectively singing body go through the same multiple motions. We need to take into account this structural divergence between mystical bodies as a collective assembly and as an interplay of individual voices when we try to explore their different functions.

With the obvious asymmetry that sets apart (normally recorded) singing voices from the more complex bodily involvement of listeners who copy them, I associate an accentuated impression, perhaps even a desire on the listener's side, of getting lost in another voice. The activation of the listener's voice may be a physical condition and an opening for this feeling of being overwhelmed by other voices—but the spectrum of physical resonance that the listener feels goes far beyond it. Are these effects powerful enough to provoke the wish or the illusion on the listener's side of becoming a different body, perhaps even a different person, not only in the physical sense? Such cultural theory questions always tend to opt for the most extreme answer. Based on my own experience, however, I think it would be an exaggeration to say that singing along with famous individual voices leaves us with fantasies of full self-substitution. We enjoy being temporarily carried away but normally leave open a way to return to our own everyday life and identity.

In 2006 I received an invitation from the Austrian government to give one of the public lectures for the celebration of Mozart's 250th birthday in Vienna and was too vain to decline, as I should have, simply for lack of competence. To make things worse and already on my way from the hotel to the Albertina, a beautiful downtown venue where I was supposed to speak, I had the bad idea to listen, via earphones, to Janis Joplin's rendition of "Me and Bobby McGee." As always, I was absorbed by her voice and subsequently had a difficult time focusing on the conversation with my hosts and, above all, on the opening parts of the lecture. The problem was not that I felt carried away into a musical world very alien to Mozart's or into the illusion of embodying Janis Joplin. Rather, and for quite some time after I had stopped listening to the song, I sensed an unusual openness in my perceptions of the Albertina building and the audience I was facing, an openness that became detrimental to my intellectual and rhetorical concentration. This state of turning to the world with diverse, not exclusively physical resonance on different levels, and potential lack of focus, is what I typically experience in the aftermath of exposure to strong individual singing voices.

If powerful voices thus ultimately trigger, for a limited time, a disposition of general excitability, more than a dynamic of personal identification with the singing voice, this may account for the lack of a particular type of reaction when we accompany the recorded voices of singers who are no longer alive—although they may still transport us back to the artist's particular historical moment. In principle, the impact of dead speakers' voices is restrained to their physical qualities. By using biographical or historical knowledge and by paying a high degree of attention to lyrics or even to details of pronunciation, we can of course arrive at an attitude where listening to a voice from the past becomes an act of immersion and an impression of being in the middle of a different world. I sometimes enjoy Edith Piaf's chansons as auditive illustrations of a mood characteristic to French postwar existentialism or hear early hits by Elvis Presley as the presentification of an atmosphere that permeated the United States during Cold War times. And yet such explorations of otherness remain on the periphery of our most intense singing along moments whose impact rather cuts short the distance between us and remote historical or cultural worlds.

We should not close the analytical focus on behaviors of singing along without some thoughts about the practice of karaoke, although, strictly speaking, it does not belong to those uses of our voice that copy and accompany other voices. The Japanese word "karaoke" has two roots: "kara" for "empty" and "oke," as an abbreviation of "okesutora" (i.e., "orchestra"); it was originally applied to situations in popular culture where recordings substituted for the presence of live orchestras in accompanying voices (mostly because of the expense of orchestras). "Empty" thus stood for the absence of a real orchestra. What primarily Japanese entertainment specialists and engineers have been developing since the 1960s and what we still call a "karaoke machine" today is, by contrast, a media environment consisting of several components: recorded orchestra or band music pieces that normally accompany songs; visual projections of their lyrics; acoustic memories, we have to presuppose, among the people who want to sing along; and microphones, frequently handed to them in their adopted role of protagonist singers. These components form an apparatus that enhances the individual voices' copying of preexisting songs without the sounds of these songs turning into physical reality. The physical "void" in karaoke and its often sophisticated "machines" is indeed the absence of the voice to be copied, no longer the absence of an orchestra.

From a purely physical perspective then, the voices of those who are doing karaoke replace songs that do not become present as sound sequences, although these people doubtlessly "sing along" what they remember from having heard the now- absent songs. Mystical bodies, by any means, cannot emerge here because there is only one real body in play. But what makes the specific fascination of karaoke different from copying and from accompanying recorded voices that are acoustically present? To my knowledge, no consensual answer to this question exists. One guess is that, due to the absence of the original recorded voices, karaoke singers do not feel overwhelmed by what they barely remember and thus have more freedom and space to become, for a period of time and always starting out with their own voice, people different from what they are in their everyday lives. On another level, and not necessarily incompatible with the supposed effect of embodying alternate personalities, karaoke singers may reach such a degree of bodily and mental openness to their surroundings that they are no longer attached to other voices and thus are potentially unlimited. How very strong such excitability can become in karaoke becomes clear from its documented tendency to expand the duration of singing into marathon formats and also to never fully control the situation, running the risk of the karaoke turning violent.

What I also find relevant for the debate about karaoke-specific fascination is the contrast between the place it occupies in Asian popular culture—from South Korea to China and Taiwan, to Japan, with an extension to the Philippines—as opposed to its rather marginal status in Western contexts. While, since the late twentieth century, karaoke has become available worldwide in urban settings, its regular practice is more of an idiosyncratic choice in Europe and the Americas. Even though electronic technology now offers versions of karaoke singing at a modest price level, in Asian cultures it has remained connected to "gentlemen's clubs," whose customers pay large fees for present-day offers in the geisha tradition. Customers are entertained through games, songs, and dance performed by beautiful women, and, contrary to a predominantly non-Asian understanding, such activities are not expected to lead to sexual contact—at least not immediately or not always. Instead, playing, singing, and dancing with geishas offers an escape from professional everyday behavior and an intransitive excitability in terms of sensual and spiritual appeals that are similar to the mood in which singing along often leaves us. This disposition has a value, a prominence, and a breadth in Asian cultures that Western observers easily underestimate—and thus could be the reason for the uneven representation of karaoke globally.

We have associated such openness to the world with a connection between individual voices and the particular type of sociability that emerges from them. Now, while I insisted on its distance from the process of joining a collective body through the mediation of voices, two basic situations of singing along also develop next to each other. Japan is not only the great nation of karaoke, but it also displays, most visibly in the country's professional baseball league, a particularly sophisticated culture of singing rituals for stadiums. Built in 1924 between Osaka and Kobe, Koshien Stadium, where the Hanshin Tigers have been playing baseball since 1935, is the sport's official "sanctuary" due to a repertoire of collective fight songs that include complicated choreographies cultivated by the local crowd. The songs are adapted to each situation of the game and probably attract more spectators than the Tigers themselves. Using our voices to sing along with others, both collectively and individually, initiates and unfolds flavors of intensity in our relation to the world that may not be available otherwise.

───── FOUR

Voices in History

LIVING THROUGH
ONTOLOGICAL DISCONTINUITY

WHAT MOST ATTRACTS ME ABOUT the past, quite naïvely, is that I can conjure up eminent figures from remote times in an almost three-dimensional way, based on documents that activate my imagination. "Hearing" the protagonists' voices is part of the process, although we hardly find any historical traces for this dimension of human existence—and not only because sound recording only became available in the late nineteenth century. Descriptions of individual voices are astonishingly scarce altogether, and those that do exist are vague. About Julius Caesar, perhaps the most emblematic historical hero in Western culture, I found just one pertinent sentence in Suetonius's otherwise colorful portrait of Caesar's style on the political and military stage: "He is said to have given speeches in a high-pitched voice with impassioned action and gestures, which were not without grace." I am reluctant to adopt this assessment, because this reference, which is already weak due to its admitted reliance on hearsay, contradicts the strong, masculine voice of Caesar that thrives in my imagination.

My impression of the voice of Otto von Bismarck, the Prussian creator of the German nation-state after 1871, has gone through a transformation in the opposite direction. While Bismarck was endowed with an unusually tall and imposing body, some historians have mentioned how unhappy he felt about his "piping voice" (*Fistelstimme*). In 2011 an early sound recording of less than a minute's length was discovered. Theo Wangemann, an assistant of Thomas Alva Edison, had made the recording during his 1889 visit to Europe where he met Bismarck. This artifact is surprising for two reasons. First, the Iron Chancellor responded to the invitation of having his voice eternalized on a wax cylinder by quoting prosodic texts in four different languages—among them, with excellent pronunciation, an English poem and the first verses of the French national anthem. Second, and counter to the mentioned biographical information, the sound of Bismarck's voice comes through as clear, but certainly not as unpleasant, let alone embarrassing—under a thick layer of noises produced by the technical device. While this acoustic trace from the past could have become the reason for a more sympathetic impression of Bismarck, my sound imagination remained unchanged—like with Julius Caesar's voice. Why should it matter at all that we adapt our imaginations to the fragile testimony of a Suetonius quote based on another quote or to the stronger evidence of a sound recording? Would a more accurate knowledge about the voices of Caesar or Bismarck improve our understanding of the roles they played in their worlds? Would it help us to better grasp those worlds at large? Why should we care about the historical truth of voices?

This indeed is the philosophical, or, more precisely, the epistemological and ontological question that will lead us through this chapter. Are voices, especially voices in their physical individuality, among the phenomena relevant for the type of thinking that we refer to as "historical"? To arrive at an initial answer and without following the most sophisticated debates among theorists of history about the concept grounding their field, I highlight the main implications of this question in its general intellectual and academic use. Ever since the emergence of the so-called historical worldview around 1800, we assume that there are no phenomena that escape their faster or slower transformation under the influence of time; among such transformations, we consider "historical" those that can only be described and thus implicitly explained by narratives; we mostly associate such narratives with human action and behavior; and we normally expect historical narratives to contain stages that appear irreversible and come together in the effect of a plot-like plausibility, although it is difficult to philosophically conceptualize such anticipations.

Seen from this angle and focusing on the corporeal component within the knot of the voice, pertinent traces from the past should of course be audible and therefore would seem to be largely incompatible with history (and not only because we lack sound recordings from before the late nineteenth century). At the same time, it seems unlikely that individual occurrences of what Roland Barthes subsumed under the concepts of the "grain de la voix" and of the "géno-voix" can ever be put together in a narrative trajectory. The assumption is based on the self-evident premise that irreversible transformations of the human body take place exclusively in the range of evolution and not within that of history. The fifth section of Hegel's *Phenomenology of the Spirit* points to an ontological ground for this epistemological difference.[1] While in his view the World Spirit mediates between life as a principle and individual human actions by establishing a level that gives to the actions in their temporal sequence an overarching background of regularity and even of logic, such a mediating level does not exist between life in general and individual human bodies. Ontologically distant from the Spirit, human life as bodily nature therefore, says Hegel, "has no history and falls from life in general immediately into the singularity of existence, meaning that the determinate lively moments assembled in this reality will produce change [*Werden*] only through the form of random movements where each element is isolated." In other words, while the organs of individual human bodies constantly change in otherwise historical time, these changes are lacking the comprehensive dynamic and direction that Hegel associates with the Spirit as a force of mediation and with "history."

As long as we separate the voice as an organ of the human body from the dimension of meanings that it can articulate, irreversible changes mainly belong to the dimension of evolution whereas differences between states of individual voices and individual voice moments constitute a sphere of variety within otherwise historical time. As soon as we reinclude meaning (or propositional content) into our considerations, the voice recuperates a relation to history because meanings almost always emerge from, describe, and anticipate human action. Our question regarding the relation between voice and history thus confronts us again, in a particularly complex fashion, with the ontological discontinuity (body and meaning) and with the epistemological discontinuity (evolution and history in this case) that experiences the knot of the voice.

While the human voice is present in our everyday life, we cannot avoid or overcome its ontological and its internal epistemological discontinuity once we try to deal with it on a conceptual level. And this double discontinuity leads to alternative ways of thinking through the relation between voice and history. In principle, we can either deal with the voice as an organ in the context of evolution or with the voice as a medium that articulates meaning in history. Neither possibility, however, does justice to the knot of the voice in its complexity. Doing justice to it requires paying the price of epistemological incoherence, whereas epistemological coherence comes with the sacrifice of only concentrating on one of the two dimensions (either evolution or history) that make up the temporality of the phenomenon. If I opt for epistemological (and discursive) incoherence in this chapter—that is, for both evolution and for history—I do so with the goal of producing a larger number of perspectives and views regarding the knot of the voice in relation to the past. After all, in this book I am trying to broaden our different approaches to the phenomenon of the human voice rather than to reveal a single comprehensive description with complementary parts.

As if building an argument for the choice of ontological discontinuity, epistemological incoherence, and descriptive complexity in relation to "voices in history" was not difficult enough, my decision to write both from an evolutionary and a historical angle brings up a further problem. Looking at the voice within evolution, we first need to ask whether there is a decisive difference and irreversible discontinuity between voices of different animal species and the human voice. More precisely, we must address the question of what anatomical conditions may have made possible the human capacity of developing language. Once these conditions are identified, we look at a time, the time of the development of human language, that belongs to history strictly speaking but for which we have no documentary evidence. It is not immediately clear how we can write about this time—that must also have been the time when certain voice functions that humans share with animals developed their particular relationship to the exclusive meaning-articulating function of the human voice. We have already seen how some acts of using our voices without articulating meaning have a specific cultural status, and how certain functions of the human voice depend on the contrast between its meaning-related and its non-meaning-related tasks. As a crucial layer of human existence whose early history did not leave any documentary traces, the origin of the difference between meaning-related and non-meaning-related functions of the voice has frequently become the object of speculation and of mythologizing, not only in Nietzsche's philosophy but also in stories about figures like the Sirens, Orpheus, or the nymph Echo.

Regarding cultural history in the usual sense of the expression, we need to ask which of its perspectives can bring into view the knot of the voice with its different aspects. The institutional side of it—that is, history of the voice as a medium of meaning articulation and its technologies—has already been dealt with in books and inspiring collections of essays.[2] Continuing with the focus on the grain of the voice, I concentrate on those altogether rare situations in the past and on their conditions where individual voices in their timbres and individual moments became an object of interest.

The chapter thus unfolds in three different discursive levels: in the evolutionary emergence of the human voice as a knot of particular structures and functions against the backdrop of the animal voice; in speculations and mythological narratives concerning the relations between the different structures and functions of the human voice as they must have emerged in the undocumented time between evolution and history; and finally in a compact narrative about the attention given to individual voices in their bodily reality.

This heterogeneous-looking approach—with hypotheses about evolution, interpretations of foundational texts, and cultural history—is my way of dealing with the relation between history and the human voice in an exercise of working through the ontological and epistemological discontinuity that characterizes the knot of the voice. What I believe to gain by abandoning epistemological homogeneity is a wide range and a deep archive of relevant views, concepts, and potential arguments about the human voice without a single vanishing point, a range and archive of insights that I found to be both worthwhile and quite difficult to shape. In the end, the three parts should of course show more than just my own way of working through ontological and epistemological discontinuity. The chapter indeed aims to offer a varied history of traces and motifs from thinkers of the past who addressed, as a permanent challenge and in specific concentration on different phenomena of the human voice, the general discontinuity with we are all living between the bodily and the spiritual dimension of our existence. Thinking about this discontinuity is a way of living with it—but solutions to its challenges are not in sight.

For the evolutionary contrast between the voices of mammals and the human voice, I mainly rely on an essay by the primatologist Julia Fischer that combines scientific knowledge and a series of hypotheses about early cultural history in a particularly inspiring way.[3] Fischer starts out by emphasizing the broad range of anatomical and physiological features that the sound-producing organs of primates share with those of humans. This similarity corresponds to some functions performed by primate voices and human voices. They both produce spatial relations of distance and closeness, establishing the basis of what I have described as existential spaces; they both function as signs of changing hormonal states and thus become indispensable for mating and procreation; and they are both perceived as indicators for different degrees of individual body strength and of emotional states, the latter of which has frequently triggered misinterpretations of animal voices as articulating language (in reality, we are dealing here with those difficult-to-conceptualize utterances that words like "crying" or "shouting" allude to). But voices also help both primates and humans to identify individual bodies within their own species (sociologists assume that we can normally distinguish around a hundred voices without specific preparation or effort).

Different from a tradition in evolutionary studies, however, and seemingly joining a contemporary tendency in her field, Fischer insists on functional differences between the cognitive behaviors of primates and humans, while not necessarily interpreting them as a symptom of human superiority. The point of convergence in her observations on language as a specifically human behavior therefore turns out to be its independence from immediate perception—that is, an independence of language and of the mind as closed systems—rather than any particular achievements that we associate with them.

Firstly, "signals" of a language convey information—with each language having its own semantic field capable of processing perceptions of the world; the relation between language signals and their external objects of reference are arbitrary, which means: what language articulates (propositional content) remains temporarily and spatially independent of its objects of reference; languages possess syntax as different internal rule sets for the concatenation of signals through which an infinity of propositional content can be produced and expressed—although there is not one common pattern from which different forms of syntax emerge; and finally, humans convey the forms and uses of their different languages to each subsequent generation through socialization and teaching—instead of relying on language as a hereditary condition.

While this list of criteria does not contain any surprises for a reader familiar with basic linguistic knowledge, the independence of language from immediate perceptions of and reactions to the environment, as a potential common denominator, points to a degree of differentiation in the articulation of language signals that the primates' utterances do not reach and thus to the capacity of willfully using such differentiation. This explains why the decisive anatomical and physiological distinction between humans and primates for the development of spoken language must lie in connections between parts of the human brain that govern deliberate bodily movements in general and the particular neurons functioning both in the vocal organs and in the tongue. Primate species lack this specific connection and therefore remain unable to use their organs for language in the human sense.

Because a functional equivalent to the human control over the vocal organs does exist for primates in their hand movements, evolutionists have speculated that a level of "language" based on hand gestures in primates (and also in humans) could have preceded our vocal language. What argues against this hypothesis is the observation that manual gestures performed by primates have never fulfilled the criteria associated with language in the specific sense. Without any anatomical or physiological discovery to account for this functional limitation in the hand gestures of primates, their distance vis-à-vis the status of language has become a starting point for speculation. Why have primates never developed a language of gestures if, in principle, their brains could have produced sufficient differentiation in hand signals? Fischer answers this question by assuming a lack of a "theory of the spirit" (*Theorie des Geistes*) among primates, that is an incapacity of attributing "knowledge, intentions, or desires" to other members of their species—and perhaps even to themselves. Such a statement obviously can never transcend the status of a plausible hypotheses.

On the level of empirical facts, therefore, the only evolutionary difference that we can connect with the emergence of language indeed refers to the already mentioned specific relationship between human voice and the brain. This encourages us to assume that what we call the human mind or the human consciousness must have originated in the use of voice—and not in the use of any other organs. Due to the obvious lack of pertinent evidence, there is no possible basis for a historical narrative describing how the willful use of voices led to language and how the development of language and the development of the mind were inseparable. But if the function of human voices in relation to language is our best and indeed only guess for an explanation of the development of the human mind, then the voice once again appears to be a privileged object of reference to think through and to work through, intellectually and existentially, the ontological discontinuity between our mind and our body.

While I have taken Fischer's insistence on the difference between primate brains and human brains in relation to their vocal apparatus as a scientific confirmation and even encouragement for my existentially motivated focus on the voice, the true intellectual provocation of primatologist work today comes from a less mind-centered approach to cognitive performance and instead from the attempt to describe functions in animal life that are inaccessible to an anthropocentric view. The potential consequences of this new orientation regarding our understanding of what is specific about the "human condition" seem unlimited. So far—and for this book—they make me aware that thinking about the human condition along the traditional lines of a mind/body discontinuity could soon become a symptom of intellectual inertia—and I am willing to accept such a risk.

While this chapter about voices in history thus does not take up all the latest trends in research and thinking, it revisits and attempts to develop some classic views on dimensions of the voice in our existence. Dealing with evolution, I thus found it worthwhile to have a look at Charles Darwin's specific focus on the voice in his 1872 treatise *The Expression of the Emotions in Man and Animals*.[4] What struck me, compared to the view of present-day primatologists, was Darwin's option for evolutionary continuity on different levels of observation and reflection. This continuity in Darwin includes the deliberate control of the vocal organs, which, as we have seen, is the decisive point of discontinuity between animals and humans in contemporary primatology. Without any research-based knowledge available about the connections between brains and vocal organs in humans and other animals, Darwin's text mentions this potential evolutionary threshold barely in passing and as a gradual difference at most. In relation to all animals, he writes, "it is possible—but this is merely a suggestion—that the greater or less mechanical facility with which the vibrating apparatus of the human larynx passes from one state of vibration to another, may have been a primary cause of the greater or less pleasure produced by various sequences of sounds."[5]

That animals in general can "willfully" control their vocal organs was never in doubt for Darwin.

Even more central, and typical for his style of thought, are three general principles that he introduces in the opening chapter as valid "for most of the expressions and gestures used by man and the lower animals, under the influence of emotions and sensations." The "principle of expressions becoming habitual" to the degree that they fulfill certain functions; the (quite surprising) principle of "antithesis," according to which "opposite states of mind" bring forth "movements of a directly opposite nature"; and a third principle about "the sensorium strongly excited" independently of the will producing movements "which we recognize as expressive." There is no need for us to criticize these principles from a philosophical, let alone scientific, point of view. They have long since become obsolete. Giving evidence to Darwin's wish for a far-reaching continuity in evolution and supported by his conviction that longstanding habits would necessarily become hereditary, the principles did prepare and anticipate the book's "conclusion that man is derived from some lower animal form and support the belief of the specific or subspecific unity of the several races."

But while many pages of *The Expression of Emotions in Man and Animals* indeed look like a case study meant to confirm Darwin's general conception of evolution as continuity, I found a passage where the specific concentration on voices arrived at a beautiful, even moving concurrence with philosophical thoughts of his time and with ancient mythology. It mattered greatly to Darwin that we discover music not only in the singing of birds but also in the underlying emotional expressions of primates and humans. Once he had accumulated what seemed to be sufficient evidence for this view, he developed the hypothesis that singing must have preceded the human capacity of articulating speech and thus the full unfolding of the human mind:

> That animals utter musical notes is familiar to every one [*sic*], as we may daily hear in the singing of birds. It is a more remarkable fact that an ape, one of the Gibbons, produces an exact octave of musical

sounds, ascending and descending the scale by half-tones; so that this monkey alone of brute mammals may be said to sing. From this fact, and from the analogy of other animals, I have been led to infer that the progenitors of man probably uttered musical tones, before they had acquired the power of articulate speech.[6]

Looking at evolution from a philosophical angle, we can say that history presupposes the control of the human brain over the vocal organs as an evolutionary discontinuity that facilitates the development of language, and via language, the human mind. History's first twenty or thirty millennia thus are ripe for imagination and speculation, articulated both in philosophical treatises and mythological narratives that deal with the co-emergence of language and the human mind. In this process the voice doubtlessly plays a crucial role, and among its dimensions I will now concentrate on that development, with language as an emerging background, of a new status and new functions for these elementary vocal layers that humans share with primates and other mammals. While we can assume for purely logical reasons that changes in the sound functions of the voice did occur, we know nothing about their details or about their impact, which explains our lasting uncertainty about all those effects of the voice that are not synonymous with the articulation of meaning. Nobody can predict, for example, on the basis of a coherent theory, how a person's specific "grain of the voice" influences our impressions of the speaker, nor explain why singing voices normally engage us with greater emotional intensity than speaking voices.

With his thesis about the singing voice as a predecessor of the voice articulating propositional content, Charles Darwin may have inaugurated a lively discursive tradition that has continued in many variations until today. In "Josephine the Singer, or the Mouse Folk," the final tale written by Franz Kafka's before his death in 1924 and a good sixty years after Darwin's *Expression of Emotions in Man and Animals,* we encounter the motif of the archaic singing voice in a strange suspense between provocative absurdity and philosophical allegory. Josephine is a mouse who is acclaimed for her singing. The mouse community gathers around her to hear her sing, although as the text-implicit narrator repeatedly insists, they hear her voice in the same "piping" (*pfeiffenden*) tone that is typical of their own speaking. Throughout the text the narrator tries to come up with an explanation for this paradoxical reaction between spellbound fascination and sobering perception, and the only answer proposed is that Josephine's audience, despite a shared "lack of musicality," has a faint memory of singing at an existential level in the distant past:

> Is she really singing after all? In spite of our lack of musicality, we have traditions of singing; in the olden times of our people there is singing; legends tell us about it, and even some songs have been preserved, although nobody can sing them anymore. But we do have an impression of what singing is.

To explain why living mice do not sing like Josephine, the narrator evokes their "prematurely aged, earnest state of mind" through whose piping and whispering language, however, some rare impressions of "a short poor childhood" with its "incomprehensible and yet real, never quite repressed vivacity" (*Munterkeit*) can penetrate. Three elements of Kafka's text are of interest for us: once again the idea of singing as preceding spoken (in this case, "piping") language; the specific status that this background from the past gives to speaking voices (without it they would not sound like "piping" and "whistling"); and, thanks to the collective memory of singing, the ambiguous mood of mouse life between earnestness and a "remote vivacity."

Shortly after Darwin and four decades before Kafka, Friedrich Nietzsche elaborated the already-discussed horizon of hypotheses about the prehistory of human language in several drafts leading to his 1872 book *The Birth of Tragedy*. For Nietzsche too, a common, purely vocal "fundament of tone" (*Tonuntergrund*) underlies a "symbolism of gestures" (*Geberdensymbolik*), which, as the opposite principle, was heading toward a multiplicity of languages (the word *Geberde* appears here without allusion to hand or body movements). Similar to Kafka but more explicitly, Nietzsche also associates the vocal "fundament of tone" with a mood state in which pleasure and displeasure are undivided.

Most importantly from a philosophical point of view, he integrated the "fundament of tone" into a quadrangle of two mutually connected distinctions: on the one hand, there is the distinction between the non-semantic "fundament of tone" and language as "consonantal and vocal word" emerging from the "symbolism of gestures"; on the other hand, there is the distinction between the "will" as existential ground (in Arthur Schopenhauer's sense of the word) and "the entire human corporeality" (*unsere ganze Leiblichkeit*) as its articulation. The "fundament of tone" and the "will" are grounding concepts in both distinctions, whereas "corporeality" and the "consonantal and vocal word" stand for the palpable reality of human life. Now, following Schopenhauer, Nietzsche understood "will" as the one dynamic under all kinds of change and transformation, but as it was also described as "the content of music," he associated the will with music, and music with singing as the "fundament of tone." This conceptual structure and movement became the origin for Nietzsche's central notion of the "Dionysian," that is for the idea of a state of mind grounded in the will and in vocal (mostly choral) music, a state of mind capable of annihilating all forms of "individuation" and of thus bringing together again "humans with humans and even with previously alienated, hostile, and repressed Nature."

No other thinker has developed the grid of concepts connected to the voice into more directions and to a higher level of complexity than Nietzsche. There are hardly any motifs in his philosophy that cannot be connected back to this configuration emerging from his focus on ancient Greek culture where the voice occupied a position too primordial for people whose minds were shaped by writing and by books within the process of modernity. But while Nietzsche was eager to integrate all those aspects derived from the voice as music into the subsequent versions of his philosophy of life (*Lebensphilosophie*), antiquity itself had to deal with the voice from diverging perspectives in multiple mythological narratives, with an apparent preference for those functions that were detached from the articulation of meaning. These narratives offer an inspiring range of motifs and images for our speculation about the undocumented time when the process of differentiation between elementary uses of the voice and spoken language must have taken place.

76 LIVES OF THE VOICE

The Sirens—who first show up as two figures without individual names in the twelfth book of the *Odyssey* and, not necessarily as a couple, in contemporary vase painting—are the mythological characters whom we probably most associate with the attractions and dangers of a non-semantic voice. In the pictorial tradition, the Sirens have strangely hybrid bodies, with women's hair, women's faces, naked breasts, and bird-like tails and legs (which later assumed a fish-like shape similar to our image of mermaids). At least two existential ambiguities correspond to this physical hybridity. As women, the Sirens seem to arouse erotic desire, but the lower animal part of their bodies prohibits its fulfillment. More relevant for us is the double function of their voices. They first address the sailors who approach their shore with both flattery and blatant lies:

> Come hither on your way, renowned Odysseus, great glory of the Achaeans; stop your ship that you may listen to the voice of us two. For never yet has a man rowed past the island in his black ship until he has heard the sweet voice from our lips; instead he has joy of it, and goes his way as a wiser man.

The voice "from their lips," however—the voice whose irresistible charm their words describe—will not make any man "wiser" because it does not use the forms of human language. Rather the *Odyssey* describes it as a "clear-toned song" without any content, against which the enchantress and goddess Circe has already warned the hero from Ithaca, advising him to listen to it only while bound to the mast of his ship and to have the ears of his sailors sealed with wax.[7] Above all it is a voice that no word or any other form of representation would ever be able to capture or to replace. As no man can withstand the temptation of this beautiful, wordless, and perhaps bird-like song, the "heart" of Odysseus "desired to listen," and he "commanded his comrades to free him" from the fetters, which they refused to do because their master had told them what he knew from Circe: "about the Sirens" there "is a great heap of bones of moldering men, and around the bones the skin is shriveling." Unlike the Sirens' treacherous words that did not succeed in changing the hero's mind, the "clear-toned song" from "their lips" unfailingly defeats any resistance from human minds and consequently kills the human bodies falling for it. And while not all irresistible voices and their music in ancient mythology have such a fatal effect, each of them features a specific power in contrast to spoken language or to perceptive regimes that are not based on ears and voices. This is what we learn from Virgil's version of the narrative about Orpheus and Eurydice.

Orpheus possesses an amazing power over nature, humans, and even gods due to both his voice in song and to the sounds of the golden lyre that he plays (music was hardly separable from voices in ancient Greek culture). In this world's imagination, there was no greater challenge than Orpheus's attempt to bring his beloved wife Eurydice back from the Underworld to which she has been confined, after having been bitten and killed by a poisonous snake on their wedding day. Like the episode about the Sirens, the narrative has several stages showing how the strength of music overcomes increasing degrees of resistance. It begins with the sadness of Orpheus's mourning song near the site of Eurydice's death, which persuades some local nymphs to advise him to descend to the underworld to negotiate with Hades and Persephone, the king and queen of Hades. In the fourth book of "Georgics," Virgil beautifully describes how, after charming the nymphs, Orpheus's song then also enchants the ghosts of the dead in Hades who are assembled like birds on a tree:

> But he, consoling love's agony with his hollow-shell lyre,
> sang you, sweet wife, you to himself on the lonely shore
> ... he entered, and approached the dead, and their terrible
>   king,
> and the hearts, unversed in gentling to human prayers.
> But by his monody shaken from the deepest pits of Erebus
> came wispy shades, and ghosts of those deprived of light,
> as many as the birds that by the thousand hide themselves in
>   leaves
> when the evening's star or winter sleet drives them from the
>   mountains.

Impressed by his voice, Hades agrees to allow Orpheus to lead Eurydice back to earth, following the sound of his music—with the one famous stipulation that he may not turn around and look at his wife before she has reached the light of the day. Until this point of the story, Virgil has followed earlier versions of the myth that were heading toward a happy ending. The fateful moment of the glance at his beloved wife who had not yet reached the surface of earth is an invention of the Roman poet and has since dominated the narrative's tradition:

> And soon his steps retracing he had dodged every pitfall
> and Eurydice restored was coming to upper air
> following behind . . .
> when a sudden madness seized him, reckless loving—
> truly forgivable, if Hell knew to forgive:
> he stopped, and upon his own Eurydice, already at the very
>   edge of light,
> forgetful, alas! And his judgment overthrown . . . he
> looked back. Instantly
> all his labor fell apart . . .

How shall we interpret this turning point, with which we are so familiar, although it must have surprised and even shocked Virgil's contemporary readers? What does it tell us about the force of music and singing? Different from Homer in the Sirens' episode, Virgil does not explicitly deal with the contrast between spoken language and song, but with an incompatibility between sounds and glances in a love relation. To maintain its power, music seems to require an exclusivity that any visual contact will dissolve. Irresistible sounds have their conditions. If spoken language may precede or follow a wordless song but not overlap with it, love that relies on the voice does not allow for an interference of the eyes. Whether such a reading would have appeared plausible in Virgil's Rome, I cannot decide. But it converges with the impression that singing tends to exclude alternative sensual and intellectual attractions. Singing indeed seems to need distance from them.

By contrast, a lack of distance decides the fate of the nymph Echo in yet another ancient Greek tale about the voice. As a minor deity of Nature, Echo belongs to a group of female characters surrounding Zeus, the erotically promiscuous father of the gods. On one of the many occasions when Hera, Zeus' wife, becomes aware of her husband's earthly relationships and descends from Mount Olympus to confront him, Echo fulfills a special task. Being "loquacious" (*garrula*), as Ovid calls her in the third book of *Metamorphoses*, she distracts the mother of the gods in a long conversation that prevents Hera from fulfilling her plan for vengeance. Once she discovers the truth behind Echo's behavior, she curses her. From that moment on, the formerly all-too-verbal nymph can only repeat the most recently spoken words of others.

This tale is not about the wordless sounds of individual voices, as they irresistibly attract attention or erotic desire, but about vocally articulated language as a medium of interaction whose topics and stories may distract listeners from their own projects and plans. Hera was seduced enough by Echo's close words that they occupied her mind and undermined her agency. The punishment imposed by the goddess therefore looks like a hyperbolic version of Echo's particular talent. If her language had managed to absorb much of the distance vis-à-vis Hera, the curse makes it distance-less and thus identical with the words of whomever is talking before her. Without distance, however, Echo loses her appeal. When she falls in love with self-absorbed Narcissus, she cannot find a way to establish the distance necessary to become an object of erotic desire for him because she is bound to repeat his words. From the angle of voices as a metaphor for the ambiguities in the relation between the human mind and the human body, the story of Echo is a warning against losing bodily appeal in an all-involving closeness and in identification with somebody else's mind. Speaking voices run the risk of losing themselves when they conquer other minds.

Trying to collect ideas and images capable of illustrating situations of the voice in the emergence of language and human consciousness, I have largely bracketed the genre differences between philosophical treatises, modern fictional texts, and mythological narratives. Read as answers to some explicit or, according to a famous description of the myth,[8] long-forgotten questions, they have all compensated for the lack of documentation from prehistorical or early historical times by providing us with some robust and astonishingly recurrent motifs about the status and the functions of voices during that remote past. Most salient seems the motif of a non-meaning-related, purely "tonal" voice preceding vocal language that recurs, without any obvious lines of influence or mutual inspiration, in the writings of authors as diverse as Charles Darwin, Friedrich Nietzsche, and Franz Kafka. Greek mythology tends to illustrate the differences between spoken language and the non-semantic tonal voice, giving the latter irresistibly seductive powers of lethal destruction or of loving union. Virgil's version of the Orpheus and Eurydice myth, however, makes that power of the musical voice depend on a condition of undivided acoustic attention, whereas the masterful use of spoken language as a means of conversation and closeness entails a divine punishment for the nymph Echo that makes her lose all physical attractiveness. Altogether, the absence of materials to establish a modestly "empirical" trajectory for the development of the voice during the earliest times of human history has led us to a horizon of images, narratives, and implicit conceptual distinctions with considerable inspirational value for reflecting on voice-related phenomena as a paradigm of ontological and epistemological discontinuity in the human condition.

The third and now fully historical section of this chapter deals with the interest in specific tonal features of voices, with the changing motivations behind such interests, and with the descriptive levels they bring to the fore. As I said before, even this task confronts us with a scarcity and a vagueness of sources that makes it difficult to escape the long shadow of Hegel's statement about the impossibility of bringing together, on a level of conceptual coherence, subsequent moments of experience with organs of the human body.

A tentative history of attention given to individual voices may begin with the observation that early relevant texts, not only from Greek antiquity, were often produced and read under the premise of being the result of a "condensation of voices"[9] and in the hope of facilitating their reactivation as an original source of articulation. Inscriptions on gravestones, for example, frequently announced that they resuscitated the voices and sometimes even tried to copy verbal idiosyncrasies of dead persons. There is no way for us to assess whether such text-inherent presence of the voice was believed to come alive. The two epics attributed to Homer do show a certain fascination for scenes of vocal performance, but they hardly ever describe their heroes' voices in any detail. During the Hellenistic centuries, such belief in text-inherent vocal immediacy clearly turned into a stylistic convention.

In Aristotle's philosophy, though, the voice occupies an explicit and indeed fundamental place whose implications and consequences are sometimes difficult to grasp for today's reader. His *De Anima* connects the voice to the soul and adds a lengthy, for us quite surprising, comment to the effect that not only the human voice but also animal voices are evidence of the presence of a soul:

> Voice is a particular sound made by something with a soul; for nothing which does not have a soul has a voice. But many animals do not have a voice, e.g. those which are bloodless, as well as fish among those which do have blood. And this is reasonable enough since sound is a particular movement of the air. So, the striking of the inbreathed air upon what is called the windpipe due to the soul in these parts constitutes voice.[10]

I will not pursue the famously complicated philological and hermeneutic questions about the exact meaning of the word "soul" for Aristotle. Given that he sees several animal species in possession of both a voice and a soul, this meaning is probably imagined as similar but not completely equal to what we call "propositional content."

A basic distinction for different types of voices according to their physical features appears in Aristotle's *Rhetoric*:

> Now delivery is a matter of voice, as to the mode in which it should be used for each particular emotion; when it should be loud, when low, when intermediate; and how the tones, that is deep, shrill, and intermediate, should be used; and what rhythms are adapted to each subject. For there are three qualities that are considered—volume, harmony, rhythm.[11]

Among these three levels of vocal "qualities," the second, called "harmony," lends itself best to individual differentiation. Whether a voice sounds "deep, shrill, or intermediate," writes Aristotle, depends on individual bodily features, whereas "volume" and "rhythm" are open to willful modulation by a speaker. This must be the reason he pays the least attention to qualities of harmony in his attempt to identify relations of "appropriateness" between, on the one side, different contents and institutional situations of rhetoric and, on the other side, different forms of vocal performance. Vocal performance, however, never appears separate from non-acoustic registers of bodily self-presentation, where Aristotle deals in detail with facial expressions and manual gestures. *Actio* would later become the Latin word for the rhetorical category joining the voice and visual body expressions.

Both the concepts of "actio" and of "appropriateness" were central in the ancient legacy of knowledge that shaped the practice of public speech up until the eighteenth century. On a similar level of abstraction, fundamental epistemological distinctions dominate over passages of detailed differentiation in Aristotle's text. Once the notion of appropriateness is unfolded, for example, he offers readers only a few references to situations where the relation between vocal performance as action and the content of a speech have not been adequate: "Whoever pronounces soft words with a rough voice and hard words with a soft voice, will not be convincing." Above all, what sets Aristotle apart from the majority of his successors in the reflection about voices as a part of rhetoric is his consistent skepticism concerning the dimension of *actio* and its components, which he critically associates with theater and theatrical acting, rather than with the seriousness of political debate: "Those who use volume, harmony, rhythm properly nearly always carry off the prizes in dramatic contests, and as at the present day actors have greater influence on the stage than the poets, it is the same in political contests, owing to the corruptness of our forms of government." This tone of principled critique has stayed alive in the discourse about speech performance to the present day.

Four centuries after Aristotle, Marcus Fabius Quintilianus in his *Institutio Oratoria*,[12] arguably the most influential text from the ancient rhetorical tradition, took up the basic architecture of Aristotle's book. Quintilian optimistically highlighted the possibilities of improving individual performance of action and voice through guided learning, whereas Aristotle had skeptically insisted on the limits of acquiring and developing what he considered to be "a gift of nature." Under its own pedagogical mission, the *Institutio Oratoria* unfolds extensive, sometimes even confusing, differentiations between physical features of the voice. "I would not hesitate to assert," Quintilian writes, "that a mediocre speech supported by all the power of delivery will be more impressive than the best speech unaccompanied by such power" (XI: 3), and he illustrates his view with long lists of mostly positive predicates for the voice as "easy, strong, rich, flexible, firm, sweet, enduring, resonant, pure, carrying far, and penetrating" or as "correct, clear, ornate, and appropriate." Ultimately, however, this plethora of distinctions only illustrates a structure similar to those we see in Aristotle. For as rhetorical treatises functioned as instruments of teaching, they could diverge in their views about the most successful strategies of public speech and in their level of detail, but they never engaged with the concreteness of individual voices. Whenever great speakers from past or present appear in these texts, as happens occasionally in Quintilian's *Institutio*, they have a status of embodiment, living proof, or illustration for general features of competence.

Only events that failed seem to have provoked attention on individual voices in the discourse of ancient rhetoric. There was a rumor, for example, that Sophocles became the first author of tragedies who decided not to participate in their performance because his voice was too weak, and that he died from overstraining this voice by endlessly reciting the text of his *Antigone*.[13] Truly fascinating is Cicero's memory of his own physical constitution in his younger years that should have excluded him from the physical challenge of active speech practice:

> In those days, I was slender and bodily weak, my neck was stretched-out and thin: this condition and this figure, people believe, are a risk of survival, as soon as they become accentuated by a tension of the lungs. Everybody who cared about me was therefore concerned about my constant practice of speaking with the highest effort of my voice and my entire body. But I believed that I should rather accept any kind of risk than abandon my hope for personal glory as an orator.[14]

While such biographical details may attract our interest because they offer concrete descriptions rather than abstractions of typology, they do not describe physical differences between individual voices. Many of Cicero's readers must have known his voice from direct experience, and for those who did not it must have been enough to know that, despite an early bodily detriment, he had emerged as one of the great speakers of their time. Proficiency in public speaking was commonly admired and a point of interest in the human voice during Greek and Roman antiquity, and this did not require descriptions of individual voices. Once the ultimate individual success of a speaker could be assumed or even taken for granted, however, references to negative features of his voice, as we have seen in Cicero's text, sometimes became a background against which individual achievement could be highlighted.

A passage in the first book of the *Iliad*, where Odysseus appears as the greatest orator among the Achaean heroes (although some bodily movements as parts of his *actio* seem inadequate), suggests that this pattern of perception may even have preceded the emergence of rhetoric as an institutional practice and as a textual genre:

> Whenever Odysseus of many wiles arose, he would stand and look down with eyes fixed on the ground, and his staff he would hold it stiff like a man of no understanding: you would have thought him some sort of a churl and nothing but a fool. But when he projected his great voice from his chest, and words like snowflakes on a winter's day, then could no other mortal man rival Odysseus, then we were not so astonished at Odysseus' appearance.

The passage from Suetonius about Julius Caesar, quoted at the beginning of the chapter, shows a similar structure of presentation. The readers knew that Caesar had been a highly efficient speaker—in spite of his "high-pitched voice." Unlikely problems overcome in the career of a speaker were the one motif in ancient rhetoric leading to individualizing descriptions of voices.

Decisive for an understanding of the institutionally central status that human voices had in the Middle Ages[15] are two famous sentences from the beginning of the Gospel of John: "In the beginning was the Word, and the Word was with God" (John 1: 1), continued by "And the Word became flesh and lived among us, and we have seen his glory, the glory of a father's only son, full of grace and truth" (John 1: 14). "Word" (*logos* in the Greek original) stands for Spirit here, implying that, being "with God," the Spirit is primordially alien to the world.

For the world to become God's world, it thus needs incarnation as an ontological transition from Spirit to flesh, and Jesus Christ, "the glory of a father's only son," is the figure in which God as Spirit becomes "flesh and lived among" humans. The Gospel of Luke translates this abstract theological configuration into the scene of a fundamental encounter between the angel Gabriel and the Virgin Mary, where the word as Spirit becomes real through a voice:

> The virgin's name was Mary, and he came to her and said: "Greetings, favored one! The Lord is with you." But she was much perplexed by his words and pondered what sort of greeting this might be. The angel said to her: "Do not be afraid, Mary, for you have found favor with God. And now, you will conceive in your womb and bear a son, and you will name him Jesus. He will be great, and will be called the Son of the Most High."

While these sentences from Luke have always been read as an announcement of incarnation and while the angel indeed speaks in the future tense, his and Mary's words, rather than only an announcement, are the actual event of Mary's conception from God. For, facilitated by the internal complexity of the voice, these words are at the same time the Spirit and the substance of incarnation, and make thus possible the ontological transition between the Spirit and the flesh, between God and humans.

Different from Aristotle's use of the concept, Christian theology does, strictly speaking, not think of the voice as a medium to express individual souls. Rather its insistence on the voice as a transition and as a neutralization (or "sublevation") of the ontological difference between Spirit and flesh, between God and the world, constitutes the specificity of Christianity as a monotheism. One could, of course, imagine such a highly abstract theological superstructure having remained without consequences for the status of the word and for the voice in everyday life, but this was certainly not the case in medieval culture. The rule prohibiting monks from using their voices outside the monastery and, more importantly, the use of Latin instead of vernacular languages as the discourse of the Eucharist (a central religious ritual) help us understand the medieval role of the human voice.

If theology suggested that the world in its materiality had become permeated by God's Spirit since the incarnation of Christ, the rituals taking place in monasteries and in churches were supposed to allow for incarnation to reach its highest degrees in worldly reality. From the early Christian centuries on, detailed and strictly observed practices had assigned to vocal music an indispensable role in this context. Singing was the main bodily form for the faithful to participate in the ritual of the Eucharist—firstly because music, according to Saint Augustine, was considered a living condensation of the divine universe, and secondly, because singing voices made the ontological transition from the Spirit to the flesh available to the believers. The celebration of the Eucharist gave humans a possibility and an orientation to become what the divine plan wanted them to be. For rather than merely expressing the Spirit in Latin texts, singing voices functioned as an embodied repetition of incarnation. There was no margin for alternatives, let alone for individual variation. In the Gregorian chant, each believer's voice became part of the single always monophonic performance, unaccompanied by instruments. No other part of human corporeal existence therefore had a higher and a more sacred status than the voice. Singing as an event and as a renewal of incarnation transubstantiated individual bodies into the community of Christians, into Christ's mystical body.

Far from religious ritual, the rediscovery of the Middle Ages in early Romanticism against their Enlightenment reputation of a "dark" age occurred as a process of reading and reappropriation concentrated on texts that had belonged to courtly culture. This exclusive focus made it impossible to understand the status of troubadour songs and of the narratives that we call "romances" as a world of imagination emerging from aristocratic circles that sometimes emphatically stood against the coherent word order imposed upon medieval society by the Church and its clerics. The troubadours celebrated an ecstatic form of erotic encounter that they deemed to be impossible within the constraints of Christian marriage. As the human body thus escaped clerical control in their songs and in images that were probably never part of any palpable reality, it seems likely that the voice in courtly culture departed from its primary religious function of repeating the event and of embodying the concept of incarnation.

Some of the most counterculturally provocative among the troubadour songs have long been associated with the name of William IX of Aquitaine, a powerful southern French aristocrat who lived for fifty-four years around 1100 and whom the Church excommunicated twice for his deliberately eccentric behavior. Resistant to all conventional efforts of interpretation, one of the nine texts in ancient Provençal language associated with his name may well have been about a singing voice exempted from meaning—although the word "voice" does not appear in any of its eight stanzas.[16] The song begins with the explicit announcement by the text-internal author and singer that he will produce a song without propositional content: "I will make a song[17] about absolutely nothing: / it will neither be about me nor about other people, / neither about love nor about youth, / nor about anything else." Its next two verses establish a double distance from the human mind as the origin of meaning: "It was invented while I was asleep / sitting on horseback." In the second stanza we read that the singer is in no mood at all, "neither happy nor sad, / neither distant nor friendly," and that this cannot be "any other way at night / on a high mountain." The song then proceeds in an ongoing alternation between repetition and variation. Five of its stanzas cross out different semantic fields and present changing words for emptiness as a state (or non-state) of the mind, whereas the concluding stanza (*tornada*) begins by saying that the "song is made, I do not know about what" and then dissolves the genre-typical gesture of sending it to a beloved woman by mentioning an uncertain line-up of several messengers going to an uncertain destiny.

Not only from the angle of intellectual history but also on strictly philological grounds, this song has certainly nothing to do with philosophical nihilism, as some of my oversophisticated colleagues have proposed in the past. For its negations exclusively refer to the different levels of meaning, while the first and the final stanza clearly state that there "will be" a song and that it "has been done." In other words, the song describes itself as a thing, and this thing can only be its acoustic reality without propositional content; it can only be a thing whose one reality is the voice, without participation of the mind.

The idea of such an exclusively vocal performance, not to mention its potential reality, must have stood in provocative opposition to the Gregorian chant and to the concept of incarnation as transition between the Spirit and the flesh. A separation (or even a liberation) of the voice occurs from its everyday connection to meaning and from its religious connection to the Spirit. But our song also posits a voice that does not converge with any other voices; it is the voice of a person "asleep on horseback" and "on a high mountain." Whether such provocations were intentional or even political, as literary historians like to say with an unavoidable risk of anachronism, we will never know. But the "song about absolutely nothing" makes it obvious that medieval courtly culture, as a counterculture, was able to imagine and perhaps to desire a vocal performance without propositional content. Whether in the end courtly culture was truly as representative of medieval societies as its Romantic admirers like to imagine is another historical question without a possible answer.

So far, we have seen how human voices fulfilled quite different functions in classical antiquity and in the Middle Ages—that is, in two worlds that both appear coherent and well-circumscribed for us. Founded on incarnation and its repeated event, the medieval world assigned to the voice a position of bringing together, according to God's will, the faithful in one Christian mystical body, whereas ancient rhetoric gave the human voice the task of being efficient in the processing of open, everyday problems. The post-medieval centuries, by contrast, made available to humans, for the first time in Western history, a position of outside observation, that is the possibility (or at least the illusion) of seeing the world without being involved in its labors and its different orders. For the experience of voices, this outside position provided more intellectual openness, as it abandoned the premise that voices and their different features needed to occupy predefined places or functions in the world orders of those who listened to them. They could finally simply sound enjoyable or off-putting, without any further reason or explanation.

If the troubadour song about "absolutely nothing" staged a voice free of any propositional content under an anti-clerical and anti-theological affect that is hard to overlook, opera as a new form of voice presentation emerged from the late sixteenth century free of any such polemical dynamics. The pathbreaking work of Karl Ludwig Pfeiffer makes it clear that opera does not function primarily, as its fans like to assume, by achieving particularly intense expressions of feelings and of narrative content; rather, it gives highly trained individual voices a framework and an opportunity to showcase themselves almost independently of the semantics that they articulate.[18] Opera performance is thus not obligated to translate the original libretto texts into languages familiar to their audiences as these audiences listen to physically outstanding voices without having religious rituals, practical functions, and related meanings on their minds—from an outside position indeed. Unlike voices in traditional and in contemporary popular music, however, opera voices require long years of technical training, as they individually try to reach the highest sound potentials of the vocal organ, and they have therefore become part of, like the bodies of professional athletes, a growing range of events in virtuoso performance. Ultimately, as Pfeiffer suggests, opera as a genre and its virtuoso voices may owe their survival and popularity in present times to the desire for preserving and experiencing a purely physical event, in a world increasingly produced by digital codes. From this angle of preserving and redeeming an analogous dimension of existence—and certainly on a quite abstract level of historical comparison—opera voices may have an affinity with William IX's most famous song.

At the same time as opera's early stages, scholarly and educational institutions brought back the ancient rhetorical tradition with its focus on voices functioning in the context of *actio*.[19] For the first time also, the practices that treatises of rhetoric had shaped would now become the focus of reflection in the texts of those who were not necessarily interested in improving their own performance as public speakers. Among these authors, the French *moralistes* of the seventeenth century not only paid attention to voices displayed in aristocratic forms of interaction, but they also discovered pertinent aspects of the canonized texts from antiquity that had been previously overlooked due to their focus on conditions of success or failure. François de la Rochefoucauld's voice-related reflections in his *Maximes*, for example, started out with an interest in the tone of the voices that still resonated with ancient descriptions and arguments regarding the role of the human body in the context of eloquence: "There is no less eloquence in the tone of the voice, in the eyes and in the appearance [*l'air*] of a person, than in the choice of words."[20] Compared to the ancient rhetorical tradition, the decisive difference La Rochefoucauld perceived was between the tones of the voice and human feelings—not between the tones and propositional content: "All the feelings have a tone of voice, gestures, and facial expressions that belong to them, and this relation, whether it is good or bad, pleasant or unpleasant, is what makes people pleasing or not pleasing to others."[21]

While La Rochefoucauld probably still thought of the connections of tones with feelings as structurally similar or even analogous to those between specific words and specific meanings, he no longer associated them with acts of understanding. Rather, he emphasized reactions (pleasant or unpleasant) we would today characterize as aesthetic—that is, of a type of judgment beginning to spread in the age of French classicism. Specific philosophical concepts for aesthetic experience, replacing taste and, more interestingly, *un je ne sais quoi* as early references, would emerge a short century later. Outside traditional thinking patterns of rhetoric that now began to lose prestige because of their highly institutional and therefore impersonal status, observations like La Rochefoucauld's about tones of the voice in relation to feelings inaugurated a concentration on those aspects in the knot of the voice that are different from its function as a medium for meaning articulation.

Although appropriate words for such intuitions were still lacking, such thoughts about vocal sounds and inner feelings anticipated later definitions of aesthetic experience as a simultaneity of physical perceptions and non-tangible intentional objects in the human psyche. Screams, for example, were described as part of the pain or of the joy that they reacted to, not as their articulation. By way of example, if we think of texts as trying to allude to such feelings, they don't have stable elements for their representation—that is, they don't have "signifiers" belonging to the vocabularies of our languages. This if why, rather than understanding them, we sense attraction or repulsion for the vocal side of feelings and through them for the persons from whose mouths they emerge. Never before the seventeenth century were such points of reference contemplated in the functions of voices and in their judgment of human behavior.

From a perspective similar to La Rochefoucauld's, Jean de la Bruyère, in *The Characters—or Customs of This Century*, engaged in an anti-rhetorically biased critique of contemporary preaching under some of the proto-aesthetic premises to which we have been pointing.[22] The use of the voice and of other body parts according to the instructions about *actio* in classical eloquence appeared incompatible to him with the seriousness of the gospel: "The Christian discourse has become a performance of entertainment [*spectacle*]; we no longer notice that evangelical sadness lying in the soul; it has been replaced by graces of the face, by inflections of the voice, by conventions of gestures, by the choice of words."[23] And yet La Bruyère did not try to guard the gospel from vocal effects. Rather, his aim was a longing for sounds whose beauty would result from an impression of individual emotion, in the absence of strategical and rhetorical uses of the voice: "it is less eloquence than the strong breath [*poitrine*] of the preacher that has an impact and moves us. He only needs noble simplicity, but this is difficult to achieve, a rare talent indeed, that transcends the strength of most people."[24] Again, what matters here is the inseparability between true feelings and the "strong breath" as their corporeal side, and we can see, more explicitly even than in La Rochefoucauld, how La Bruyère appreciated their intertwinedness as the product of a "rare talent," of an individual talent indeed whose effects could not be reached by acquiring a specific competence.

Ultimately La Bruyère described such moments of closeness between true emotions and their bodily objectifications as "beautiful enthusiasm" capable of touching those who listen to a good and, as we would say today, to a truly "authentic" speaker: "instead of engaging in those extraordinary efforts that taint the gesture and undo the face, he will bring, thanks to a beautiful enthusiasm, conviction to the minds and concerns to the hearts."[25] In the section of his book dedicated to women, we find a confirmation for the hypothesis that the beauty of bodily effects is always an individual effect for La Bruyère—although he of course refrains from naming women who possess it: "A beautiful face is the most beautiful thing that we can experience; and the sweetest harmony is the sound of the voice of the one we love."[26] If the second clause triggers a suspicion about the beauty of a woman's voice being but a subjective projection of her lover, the distinction introduced by the following statement exempts beauty from all relativity: "Charm is arbitrary; beauty is something more real and more independent of taste and opinion."

The observation that voices are attached to human feelings and the insistence on the beauty of voices as a quality inherent to individuals and independent of all function-oriented strategies, as we have seen in La Rochefoucauld and La Bruyère, motivated their rise to prominence in debates about aesthetics in the age of Enlightenment. While rhetorical techniques and the voice's traditional epistemological context were now increasingly considered reflection of beauty and of the sublime, a supposed affinity between the voices of animals and humans became a new reason for enthusiasm. Denis Diderot considered the scream as a fulfillment of man's passionate nature and therefore as an indispensable orientation for playwrights:

> It is the animal scream of passion that must dictate to us the line that we need. The more monotonous our language turns, the less accent it has, the more we need an elementary discourse, the general voice of passion. The animal scream of human passion gives it to us.[27]

Diderot's initial interest in a specific phenomenon seen from a specific perspective—in this case, the idea of a proximity between human voices and animal voices—grew into a fascination without thematic constraints. *Rameau's Nephew*, probably his most colorful and complex protagonist, whose inspiration in real life was the socially outcast nephew of a famous composer, indeed ended up impressing Diderot's readers as a virtuoso voice performer whose talent went far beyond the expression of elementary emotions:

> He sang thirty tunes one on top of the other and all mixed up: Italian, French, tragic, comic, of all sorts and descriptions, sometimes in a bass voice going down to infernal regions, and sometimes bursting himself into a falsetto voice he would split the heavens asunder, taking off the walk, deportment and gestures of different singing parts: in turn raging, pacified, imperious, scornful.

Whether the real Rameau, whom Diderot must have met at Palais-Royal, then the center of social life in Paris, really engaged in such astonishing vocal virtuosity remains unknown. But it is important to notice that this detailed description of an individual vocal performance refers to a literary character, whereas we find few similar passages in the texts of more prosaic genres.

Altogether, aesthetic reflection and aesthetic practice became the new dominant framework for references to the human voice in the course of the eighteenth century. Admiring Diderot's work, Johann Wolfgang von Goethe wrote the first German translation of *Neveu de Rameau*, and as the director of Weimar's courtly theater, he gave particular attention to the actors' voice training and to their vocal performance. While he instructed them to adapt their voices as best they could to the characters they embodied, Goethe also promoted public recitations of texts ranging from poetry to philosophical deliberations, insisting on the display of the speakers' individual voices as a condition for aesthetic experience.[28] Largely thanks to Goethe, events of voice art (*Sprechkünste*) enjoyed a specific presence, aura, and prestige in German nineteenth-century culture, which may account for the importance of the voice, a century later, as a topic of inspiration in Charles Darwin's work and in the philosophy of Friedrich Nietzsche.

On July 18, 1877, barely eighteen months after Alexander Graham Bell had patented a device for the transmission of voices as the earliest version of the telephone, Thomas Alva Edison succeeded in recording his own voice while greeting the new day with the sound of the word "hello." Multiple steps of functional improvement and complexity quickly followed and facilitated, during the first decades of the twentieth century, the rise of the radio as the first truly "social medium" and subsequently the development of soundtrack film, with simultaneously recorded visual and acoustic impulses of perception.[29] In the early stages of this new sound technology, movie producers frequently replaced silent film actors with actors whose voices were considered to be more attractive.[30] But instead of inaugurating new ways of featuring the human voice, the sound technology did not change the cultural status of the voice as much as we might have expected. Literary authors as distinguished as Virginia Woolf and Thomas Mann seemed to have some interest in characterizing the voices of their fictional characters, while some early soundtrack films displayed strangely utopian and soon abandoned fantasies about future aesthetic effects.

We have seen how the French moralists alluded to the voice as a possible symptom for the various states of the human psyche. Ernst Cassirer's philosophy of symbolic forms with its focus on "perception of expression" (*Ausdruckswahrnehmung*) went further when he ambitiously proposed, on systematic grounds, to interpret the "physiognomy of the voice" as an embodiment "of the whole person" in her or his "subjectivity."[31] And while Denis Diderot gave aesthetic value to the "animal scream of human passion," Ernst Jünger attributed to the voice's non-semantic moments an ultimate truth value; in his ecstatic "Praise of Vowels" from 1934, inspired by Rimbaud's poem about the colors of vowels and based on a distinction between "word language" and "sound language" (*Wortsprache und Lautsprache*), he proposed that this truth value could reveal how human existence was embedded in collective destiny.[32] Although Cassirer and Jünger could hardly have diverged more in their guiding intuitions about the voice as potential physiognomy of individual character or as revealing truths about collective life, they both gave to the voice an importance that it had never received before the age of sound recording and sound transmission, an importance, however, that did not yet include a focus on individual vocal profiles.

What historical knowledge about the early twentieth century has registered as the one fatal development in the life of the voice is Fascism as a phonocentric form of politics.[33] The ideology and practice of an absolute dictatorship—attracting, assembling, and "leading" nations as collective physical bodies that Benito Mussolini first designed in post-1918 Italy—depended on his strong masculine voice and the style of his bodily performance: on the two components of *actio* in classical rhetoric. Different from ancient rhetoric though, Fascist *actio* tended to replace, more than just to supplement, propositional content shaped into arguments. There was no Fascist project of persuading, let alone of convincing, the popular "masses" to understand and embrace a political position; these masses were turned from being a potentially threatening social upheaval into a more symbolic horizon providing impressions of authenticity and authority. Mussolini's voice, and soon after him Hitler's voice, received praise and admiration above all for being "rousing" (*mitreißend*) with their individual sound profiles, which made it difficult for their parties to establish institutions for the teaching of general Fascist rhetoric based on universal principles.

From a historical angle, we can say that the voices of the first two Fascist "leaders" proved irresistible (and, in the end, lethally destructive) for millions of fellow Italians and Germans—which may well remind us of the Sirens' singing in Greek mythology. Fascism relied on meticulously staged events of vocal performance for large audiences as the core ritual of phonocentric politics, and it used recording and radio technology to multiply the numbers of listeners. Situations without such scenography, let alone conversations or interviews with central political figures, did not belong to the canonized forms of Fascist broadcasting. That Francisco Franco—who had won the Spanish Civil War between 1936 and 1939 with military support from Italy and Germany and first seemed to adopt a Fascist ideology with its specific rituals—ended up favoring different tools and symbolic legitimations of dictatorial control most likely had to do with his unappealing and often fragile-sounding voice.

Today the phonocentric rituals of fascism have become incapsulated in historical memory without the possibility of return, which is probably due to the transition from exclusively phonocentric radio to the dominance of television rather than to rising ethical standards. The attention given to human voices has undergone a profound change ever since, a change that, counter to powerful expectations around 1900, did not happen after the invention of sound recording and the inauguration of radio broadcasting. In the unfailingly intelligent opportunism of a former adherent to National Socialism, Ernst Jünger surprised the readers of his diary *Strahlungen* from 1949 with a both meticulous and subtly ironic description of Joseph Goebbels's voice, a description whose tone would have been incompatible with his "Praise of Vowels" from 1934:

> The voice of the Doktor[34] was not bluntly aggressive. It was carefully drawn out, thinly wired, disciplined. It was not the voice of the great tribunes from history who were aware and certain of their mission and their message. His performance had a deliberately chosen tone; it triggered the imagination of concentrated studies pursued during ascetic vigils. One finds this type of voice among advertising specialists, under champions of sale who come to recommend complicated insurances and who end up involving their customers in long-term payment programs.[35]

While the political impact and the aesthetic appreciation of non-virtuoso voices has probably diminished, Jünger's detailed description of a historical voice from memory reads like an overture to certain attitudes that began to dominate our reactions to voices since the mid-twentieth century. Roland Barthes's focus on "the grain of the voice" and his attempt to evoke the individual baritone voice of Charles Panzéra belong in this category. The attraction and repulsion that tones of real voices can trigger, together with their "singularity,"[36] have finally become topics of philosophical debates, as well as the vanishing of the "pathos of expression"[37] that had surrounded discussion of voices since the age of Enlightenment. And this environment is of course the historical and intellectual condition for my book. By no means, however, should we assume that its typical attitudes have arrived at the end of a historical trajectory as the revelation of a definitive Truth (or some definitive truths) about the essence of voices.

We simply are more interested in individual voices and in bodily aspects of the knot of the voice than ever before. The reasons for this change are varied and altogether opaque. As an initial trigger in this direction, I can remember the troubling ambiguity between an official, intellectual rejection and a secret fascination for the dominant voices of fascism during the post-war period. For many decades now, growing numbers of remote voices, with invisible or visible bodies, have accompanied everybody's life on the telephone, on the radio, on television screens, and recently also in Skype or Zoom conversations; this omnipresence may have made them less salient as an existential phenomenon. On the other hand, electronic communication as mostly voice-less communication has probably produced a new desire for voices as a promise of closeness and immediacy—and is indeed able to perfectly copy existing and to convincingly create body-less (and in this sense fictional) voices.

All these partly contradictory layers and dimensions of vocal behavior in the contemporary everyday world have given the knot of the voice a density that is increasingly difficult to conceptualize. As for the new attention dedicated, without any aesthetic passion or pathos, to individual voices in their physical reality, it may have developed together with the expansion of a flat mode of individuality free of aura and ambition, with a type of individuality that diversifies and loses itself in endless combinations and crossroads of reading, viewing, and listening to our computer screens. Different from the great age of television when certain popular programs were regularly able to unite entire societies, no two persons today pursue the exact same images and words during a day in front of their laptops. We have thus become hyperbolically individual, and while we do not attach any pride or self-glory to this condition, it may well have transformed our patterns of social perception toward higher degrees of attention.

Our current interest in individual voices with their tonal specificities could be the latest of those different common denominators that have shaped voice experience for two-and-a-half millennia in Western culture. They began with the focus on efficiency in ancient Greek and Roman rhetoric, were followed by the voice as an event of incarnation mediating between the divine Spirit and human flesh during the Middle Ages, and later made the voice a core object of aesthetic experience since early modernity. Occasionally voices also became the fulfillment of a desire for an analogous experience of the human body independently of mind and meaning.

But none of these dominant voice configurations from the past ever brought forth a concentration on individual physical features. Such a general absence of attention for individual voices may have been a consequence of their attachment to propositional meaning. For in an average interaction, we cease to register individual features of a voice as soon as we have identified the meaning that it is supposed to convey. "Reading a face," by contrast, never allows us to arrive at a comparable certainty about what it may express because such a reading does not rely on language with its stable semantic dimensions—and is thus an always potentially endless process. Meaning, by contrast, pushes sound perceptions into the background of our experience and memory. If today we turn to voices and their sounds with a greater sensitivity for their individuality, this may indicate that electronic communication has partly liberated them from the function of meaning transmission.

The four historical stages of voice configuration that we have described—that is, rhetorical efficiency, theological incarnation, aesthetic aura, and the present focus on individual layers of sounds—do not come together, in the context of evolution, in what anybody would call "a history." None of those frames from the past presupposes its chronologically previous stage as an achievement or as a developmental step on which to rely and to build. This chapter's concentration on voices and on the forms of attention given to them in the past thus proves Hegel right. We have not discovered a continuous line of human action going through their different moments, a line of human action that makes the Spirit and its transformations visible, as Hegel would have said. Being the past of an organ, the voice's past "falls apart' into instances of "singularity" whose traces tend to recede into the background of our experience. For all of these reasons, it makes sense to say that the voice has no history.

And yet we find it difficult to resist the urge of exposing ourselves to the ontological discontinuity that goes through the knot of the voice—probably more so in our everyday behavior than in philosophical reflections. I have described the sequence of reactions to this urge as the process of "working through" an existential challenge, but this formula is only adequate if we abandon the expectation that the different stages of thought will ever reach an endpoint of clarity or definitive insight. In their temporal succession, the impulses coming from the voice remind me of Martin Heidegger's concepts of "history of Being" (*Seinsgeschichte*) and "self-unconcealment of Being" (*Selbstentbergung des Seins*) as its core event. "Self-unconcealment of Being" refers to instants where Being, that a state of phenomena independent of any specific human perspective, is showing itself and comes to the fore, against the surface of "beings" (*Seiendes*) as the tissue of our everyday life that consists of experience under different particular perspectives. According to Heidegger, to be present in events of self-unconcealment of Being is principally possible within human life, but we cannot expect or achieve it at any given moment. It has to happen by itself, and we must let it happen without any attempts of provoking it. This is the attitude that Heidegger calls *Gelassenheit* ("serenity," "composure") and that he describes as a necessary condition—not as a guarantee—for self-unconcealment of Being to occur.

Like the configurations and moments of the voice in the past, such events of self-unconcealment of Being as events of Truth do not come together in historical trajectories. The other possible affinity between *Seinsgeschichte* and the past of the voice is more uncertain and has a potential for greater existential importance. If the word "Being" indeed refers to a reality free of perspectives whose unconcealment humans should not expect and cannot achieve, our experience of voices sometimes seems to suggest a hope for transient moments of palpable truth, impossible to conceptualize, to repeat, let alone to hold on to. Such moments of palpable truth can be devastating. The allusion of the Sirens' episode to the irresistible attraction of a song that no human has ever resisted and survived makes up its chilling fascination. But I also sense an affinity between Being unconcealed and the individual grain that we hear and can never fully grasp in the voices of admired or beloved others.

Thinking and working through the knot of the voice, in history and broad variation, has been a way of confronting the ontological discontinuity in which we are living as bodies with a mind. It has not produced stable concepts or new layers of knowledge. In the best case, working through the ontological discontinuity of voices leads to brief impressions of existential evidence, beyond or below our practices of representation.

———— FIVE

Voices and Imagining
ON THE VERGE OF AGENCY

BESIDES JUST THE SOUND of my father's voice, what truly made up a painful presence in my childhood and adolescence were the dark images of potential humiliation, tension, and fights in our family life that his voice invariably unleashed. Such triggers, however, do not only accompany exception situations of trauma or aesthetic intensity. Imagination provoked by voices fulfills a central role in everyday communication. For as we often don't find ourselves in an immediate sensory contact with the objects to which we are referring, we must imagine them to know what we are talking about. While the predominant everyday function of voices or of writing presupposes that the imagery produced remains under the control of our minds and their intentions, dynamic streams of imagination provoked by sounds and timbres of individual voices can also escape volition and understanding. This is one of the reasons why we find some voices irresistibly attractive and others inevitably off-putting, without feeling able to say or do much about it. The "animal scream of passion" that so fascinated Denis Diderot and his readers constitutes an intermediary case among the imagination-related phenomena in the knot of the voice. Unlike our reactions to the mere sound of individual voices, we do not ignore that somebody who screams wants to express a specific emotion, while at the same time we let such non-linguistic utterances bring to the fore imaginings that, as we know, nobody intended.

If the sound of voices gets our imagination going in diverse ways and on multiple levels, we can also use imagination to recall the sounds of individual voices or to try to invent voices that we have never actually heard. This second relation between imagination and voices—evoking voices as objects of imagination—appears to be in psychological asymmetry with our experience of perceived voices activating imagination. Whereas we frequently struggle to stop or at least to repress the powerful streams of imagination unleashed by the sounds of voices, efforts to recall or to make up voices in our mind often are disappointing, as if our will could not quite reach imagination and make it work. Finally, there are auditory hallucinations, products of acoustic imagination no doubt, yet products of imagination that go back neither to the will nor to perception and are mostly assigned to the horizon of psychiatric pathologies. But, as it seems impossible to set aside, on a conceptual basis, auditory hallucinations from the voices of gods or from the voice of conscience that many of us hear even if we have no desire to hear it, we should include auditory hallucinations and transcendental voices in the same typological section.

In these three different relations with imagination, the human voice once again strikes us as a disorderly topic. The connections that we have identified—imaginings triggered by the sounds of individual voices, individual voices conjured up by willful acts of imagination, and imagined voices that exist independently of perception or the human will—are at the same time separate from one another and intertwined in complicated ways. Making things even more difficult and obliging us to abandon the use of everyday words that I have so far employed, we quite astonishingly cannot rely on one philosophically consensual concept that would do justice to all the different layers and functions of imagination in the core of human existence. As we step into largely uncharted intellectual territory, therefore, my analysis of the relation between voices and imagining will proceed along a phenomenological route of patient self-observation, introduced by the development of a grounding notion of imagination that is open enough to address its three different relations with the voice.

To begin, besides a comprehensive concept of imagination, we also need, as a second philosophical foundation, a hypothesis about the specific status of auditory imagination in contrast to the modalities of imagination based on other senses. This is necessary for our understanding of imagination triggered by voices, of voices conjured up by acts of imagination, and of voices imagined independently of perception or will. Within this complicated trajectory (reflecting again our disorderly topic), I will pursue, as a recurring aspect and a potential point of convergence in the different interactions between voices and imagination, the role of voices as a challenge to human control, volition, and agency.

The word "imagination" refers to the capacity of the human mind to produce content without being synchronized to acts of perception outside our consciousness. Although all content of the human mind, all "intentional objects," and all representations may ultimately derive from perceptions, we do not necessarily find ourselves in an actual process of perception each time that we activate intentional objects. Whenever this is not the case, the intentional objects have the status of the imaginary. From the angle of non-synchronicity with perception, and counter to the implication that the everyday use of imagination is exceptional, acts of imagination are thus quite central in the normal functioning of our minds. We of course have representations of a sunny landscape, a loud song, or a dry wine while we are physically perceiving them, but the more the interactions are mediated by language, the less this is the case—and the more we rely on imagination.

There is a frequent misunderstanding about the etymology of the word "image" as the root of "imagination," but acts of imagination do not necessarily come from visual impressions; they can also come out of their acoustic, tactile, gustatory, and olfactory equivalents (and any other human senses). Further, if non-synchronicity with actual perception remains the primary criterion for what the imagination does, then everything we call memory belongs to this dimension even if everyday language tends to dissociate imaginings as future-oriented and memories as originating in the past.

Another aspect of imagination concerns the origin of the impressions it projects. Can we only imagine what we have previously perceived (which would ultimately mean that each individual imagining is coextensive with an individual's repertoire of memories) or can imagination produce impressions without such antecedents? The prevailing opinion opts for the first possibility and thus explains why Jean-Paul Sartre, in his treatise *The Imaginary* from 1940 (probably the most influential publication ever on the topic), stated that "we will never learn anything new" from imagination.[1] While I principally agree with Sartre's position, I do find it plausible to assume that acts of imagining can combine elements from different previous moments of perception in innovative, collage-like ensembles. Finally, we should mention that the activity of imagining to a large extent consists of supplementing and completing representations based on actual perceptions. For if such representations are mostly fragmentary, as Sartre observes (based on an actual perception, we indeed can always only "see" one side of intentional objects), we normally end up experiencing them three-dimensionally or in their totality thanks to imagination adding the aspects missing in actual perception.

So far, I have described imagination through its different features and as a central capacity and activity of the human mind. A different look at the phenomenon, mostly connected to the words "imagery" and "imaginary," brings into view the reservoir of impressions that acts of imagination can evoke.[2] Proposing an understanding of "fiction" as a discourse based on the imaginary (as opposed to discourses claiming to be based on actual perception), the literary theorist Wolfgang Iser repeatedly characterized the imaginary as a "featureless and inactive potential."[3] To unwrap the predicate "featureless" in this context, I will initially use the notion "substance of content" developed by the Danish philosopher of language Louis Hjelmslev.[4] Applying the elementary linguistic "sign" concept as a distinction and connection between a "signifier" (expression) and a "signified" (content) by applying the Aristotelian distinction between form and substance to its two sides, Hjelmslev enables us to think of "substance of content" as a dimension in our mind where different semantic and sensory impressions coexist without forms of internal distinctions and external shapes (here lies the proximity to Iser's "featurelessness"). By understanding the imaginary as substance of content, I highlight its status as a potential—a potential that can be activated and shaped according to different specific situations. At the same time, "substance of content" corresponds to my certainty of "hearing" the complex singular tones of specific voices in one synchronic way, without having to remember them in the temporal forms of their performance and without distinguishing between their different internal levels and dimensions.

In addition, most reflections about the imaginary assume an existential closeness to the human body, although they hardly ever make such intuitions fully explicit. As long as we think of the imaginary as an unformed potential, this would have to be a closeness to the human body as an elementary, pre-voluntary framework of lived experience, rather than a closeness to the body as a circumscribed object of experience (a closeness to the body that Edmund Husserl called *Leib* as opposed to the body as *Körper*). In many of his seminars, Jacques Lacan observed that what energizes erotic desire, and the not-only-visible impact it has on body organs, is the imaginary in this sense, more so than actual perception.[5]

Why would such existential closeness between the imaginary and bodies as the elementary framework of lived experience matter? I believe this intuition converges with the impression that effects of the imaginary—and perhaps effects of the acoustic imaginary specifically—frequently happen outside the mental reach of human agency and thus perhaps in connection with predominantly physical processes of human existence. At the same time—and concluding our conceptual unfolding of "imagination" and "the imaginary" in their different dimensions—we should underline that not all their aspects escape or even resist agency. If Wolfgang Iser insists that the imaginary as a "featureless potential" requires acts or occasions of activation to yield intentional objects as objects of experience in our mind, many of these activations indeed trace back to individual intentions. Literary authors, painters, and composers all quite deliberately—though not always successfully—try to evoke visual, acoustic, tactile, or other sensory impressions in their minds.

In contrast to that willful evocation of impressions, we often unsuccessfully struggle to block powerful and obsessive imaginings that voices initiate in our psyche. Out of our control, these streams triggered by individual voices are by no means only acoustic. Everybody knows how both intentional objects emerging from actual perception and intentional objects activated from the imaginary often lead to what we call "associations": the sometimes energetic and at other times elusive sequences of impressions in our mind. Independently of their primary intentional object, such streams can switch between different sensory modalities, which makes them a particularly pertinent object for comparative observations about the specific status of acoustic impressions and, within this focus, for the specific status of voices. A main criterion for the distinctions between different sensory modalities lies in the possibility, or even in the likelihood, for each of them to transform into other modalities. While it would be an exaggeration to speak of the regularities that such transitions show as a "grammar," I believe that they proceed in similar ways in most people's minds.

Visual impressions from actual perception or from the imaginary, almost synonymous with "images" in the everyday sense of the word, seem to be the one modality that allows for transitions into all other modalities. The picture of a body can trigger the acoustic imaginary of a voice belonging to it and the tactile imaginary of a handshake or an embrace; a photograph of a piece of fried fish can evoke a particular olfactory impression and a particular impression of taste. By contrast, intentional objects in the tactile modality may produce visual or taste impressions, although it is unlikely or perhaps even impossible that they transform into olfactory or auditory impressions (readers of Braille, however, may well be able to evoke both visual and auditory impressions from their tactile perceptions). Altogether the non-visual sensory modalities have differently limited horizons of association, even if Marcel Proust's proverbial madeleine episode at the beginning of *In Search of Lost Time* demonstrates that memories of taste (which are different from immediate perceptions of taste) can conjure up multisensorial impressions of entire worlds from the past.

Compared to the other senses, intentional objects in the acoustic modality—among them, human voices above all—evoke visual and tactile impressions, impressions that I often find particularly lively and sometimes indeed irresistible in the literal sense. Although seeing a person may not necessarily make us imagine a voice, it is difficult to think of a telephone conversation where the other voice does not provoke an image of the person suggesting a correspondence with its sound. And doesn't the widespread obsession with erotic voices imply that there is an equally strong, truly irresistible association between voice impressions and tactile impressions? This may have to do with the fact that acoustic perceptions are always and inevitably also tactile perceptions because they are based on sound waves that hit our bodies. Without trying to single out and give a superior status to vocal impressions, we may speculate that their liveliness and the long chains of associations they can launch were a decisive motivation for the emergence of the German word *Stimmung* (literally "voiceness") that refers to a simultaneity of multisensory impressions with particular intensity and homogeneity, like the *Stimmung* of a festive celebration or a beautiful landscape, of a colorful artwork or a cherished personal memory.

Within the comparisons between acoustic and other sensory modalities in the imaginary, I would like to bring up one further, specifically complicated aspect. Acoustic representations are obviously connected to the status of time objects—that is, to the status of phenomena that only exist in their temporal unfolding (linguistic performance, music, and any type of movement are all time objects in this sense). Elements of visual representation, by contrast, can but mostly do not come in such temporal structures, which also appears to be true for tactile, gustatory, and olfactory impressions. They normally remain one-moment effects for us. As a general rule in the realm of actual perceptions, all intentional objects seem to have a capacity of occasionally turning into time objects—but only the perception of acoustic phenomena occurs predominantly in this form. If we praise a wine for its "great finish," we imply that, almost counterintuitively, a gustatory impression sometimes assumes the form of a time object. On the other hand, I have already mentioned how representations of some individual voices that we have perceived—again counterintuitively—can appear contracted into one internally complex tone, a complex tone that we are convinced to hear, while we are not able to produce this same effect for all voices that we remember.

Mostly, however, we perceive and try to imagine voices in the form of time objects. By contrast, as I said, the primary (not the exclusive) form in which activated elements from the imaginary generally articulate themselves in our mind seems to be synthetic and thereby non-temporal. It may be due to this difference between imagination in general producing synthetic impressions and acoustic perceptions having the primary form of time objects that we find it more difficult to actively imagine acoustic impressions than to actively imagine visual, tactile, gustatory, and olfactory impressions. The mastery of composers may well have to do with the exceptional capacity of imagining instrumental music or songs as temporal objects against the challenge of the synthetic form as primary form within the imaginary.

Probably due to an elementary tension between the general form of imagining and the basic structure of acoustic perception, we often either "hear" complex, synthetic tones when we succeed in imagining and remembering individual voices—or we notice that they remain silent. Silence has been the case with my mother's voice. Since I started to think about voices with some serious concentration, I have tried experimenting by voicing sentences frequently spoken by my mother that I could remember in their form as temporal objects without a vocal impression. I will not say that the experiment completely failed, but it confirmed the particular difficulty of imagining sounds for voices that are primarily silent in our memory. Thinking along these lines about the relation between time as primary form of voice perception and the predominantly synthetic form of activating elements from the imaginary brings to mind two different and yet related limits of our agency over imagination: it clarifies why we cannot control dynamic streams of impressions and associations triggered by individual voices, and it reinforces why it is so difficult to imagine voices that we do not immediately hear.

Having reviewed the complementary notions of imagination and the imaginary in their multiple dimensions and having identified what may be particular about voice impressions within the different sensory modalities of the imaginary, we now turn to conceptual distinctions, intuitions, and open questions; these may serve as guidelines for our analysis as we try to extract further relevant observations by focusing on the three different intersections between voices and imagining: on streams of imagining triggered by voices, on acts of imagination conjuring up voices, and on voices as an imaginary independent of the human will.

For streams of imagining triggered by the perception of voices, we have seen how they usually start with particularly strong visual or tactile impressions; they then often continue in chains of association, by potentially transforming into the other sensory modalities of the imaginary, and it is typically complicated to control them. Focusing on historical cases, personal experience, and previous theoretical insights, I try to illustrate and to differentiate what I have said so far about sounds of individual voices and the imaginary that they evoke, abstaining from all those phenomena that, different from individual sounds of voices, linguists identify as elements of a dialect or of an idiolect, because they are subject to efforts of deliberate change.

In his polemical essay from 1778 "On Physiognomy: Against the Physiognomists—for the Promotion of Human Knowledge and the Love of Humanity," the philosopher of nature Georg Christoph Lichtenberg described a voice-related self-experiment with an attention to detail and a personal passion that has over time gained more resonance among German intellectuals than the text's original argument.[6] Himself a victim of stunted growth and well aware of the consequences of this condition, Lichtenberg based his critique on the contemporary physiognomists' claim that it was possible to read human faces as the expression of moral states and qualities; this led to a broader debate concerning the conclusion that ethically relevant insights based on different objectifications of physical life could not exist. If his main point therefore was to show that a person's bodily appearance was an unreliable source for extrapolations about her character, Lichtenberg also argued, with some other problematic assumptions, that listening to an individual voice would always allow the projection of an accurate body image.

Within his argument, some implicit beliefs and casual remarks turn out to be particularly important. When he states that we are almost always surprised and mostly disappointed when we eventually see the real bodies that, trusting the perception of voices, we had previously imagined, Lichtenberg seems to presuppose that we cannot help producing such pictures: "Whoever has traveled on a stagecoach at night, and has gotten to know people in the dark whom he had never seen before, will have projected an image of them during the night and feel deceived in the morning." To further illustrate his point, Lichtenberg comes back to an experiment that he had undertaken several years before writing his essay against the physiognomists. For many years, he had heard the "screaming voice" of a night watchman in his hometown of Göttingen, for this voice would wake him up throughout the night "telling him the hour." Having never seen the watchman, he tried to describe and draw an image of his body: "the voice provoked the picture of a tall, haggard, but altogether healthy man, with a longish [*länglich*] face, a hooked nose, unbound straight hair, and a slow, solemn way of walking." Reading this sentence, we see a three-dimensional figure before us, the appearance of an entire body indeed, and this appearance presents itself as independent of any specific perspective.[7]

When Lichtenberg finally met the night watchman, however, he not only realized that the product of his imagination by no means corresponded to what the man actually looked like, but he noticed that, influenced by an individual voice, his imagination had created a strangely eccentric picture in comparison to the average looks of the real man: "he rather was of median height, friendly and direct, and had his hair bound together in a small braid." Astonished both about the discrepancy between the real night watchman and his own imaginary and about the tendency to project such a vivid image, Lichtenberg searched for the reasons and for the origin of his reactions; he found answers in previous moments of perception and imagination during his life, thus confirming the view that our imaginary does not really invent unprecedented impressions. He remembered that in his childhood he had seen a particularly tall man with a voice as deep as the night watchman's, that some features of the imagined man's face came from reactions to his own adolescent readings of ancient Greek mythology, and that, during his university years, he was friends with a student whose solemn walk he had transferred to the picture of the night watchman in his imaginary.

Together with the three-dimensional dynamism of the imagined picture, both Lichtenberg's conviction about the inevitability of imagining a body that one cannot see under the influence of its voice and about the origin of such pictures in previous perceptions indeed converge with some of our more abstract speculations about voices and imagination. His main fascination certainly remained the unreliability of such voice-based projections, in his case the sobering realization that "he had honestly not guessed a single detail" of the night watchman's real face and appearance. Does this mean that imaginings based on the perception of human voices never have any reality value? One possible answer to this question goes back to what I said before about our reactions to erotically appealing voices (and, by analogy, about voices that we find repulsive) and requires that we shift, for a reality criterion, from the correspondence between projected images and true appearances to a possible consensus in the reactions to individual voices.

While there are always exceptions, most people will agree about whether they find individual voices either appealing or repulsive. How can we explain this tendency toward consensus? If it is correct to assume that voice perceptions produce primary reactions both in the visual and in the tactile modality of the imaginary, it seems obvious that, different from Lichtenberg's guess about the night watchman's appearance, we find voices attractive or repulsive based on the tactile imaginary. We can imagine how it would feel to embrace the body of somebody whose voice we hear, what a handshake would be like, or whether we would want to be in a conversation with somebody and his voice for a longer stretch of time. The third example makes it clear how, different from visual perception, being exposed to a voice invariably activates our tactile perception because, unlike visual perception, sounds do hit the surfaces of our bodies.

We not only imagine what an acoustic perception may announce for the tactile modality, but at the same time a tactile perception occurs on our skin and in our ear. And although reactions to this real feeling may diverge, they produce broader consensus than we are used to for the visual modality. This obviously also applies to both pleasant and unpleasant voices. I have, for example, never heard of or read about anybody remembering Martin Heidegger's strained and slightly squeaky voice as appealing, not to mention his unsuccessful and therefore embarrassing efforts to repress the southwestern accent in his German pronunciation. However, ever since his early years as a teacher, large numbers of students attended Heidegger's lectures and admired him as "the king of philosophy"—in full awareness of his unpleasant voice.

Returning one final time to my father's voice, it was not at all physically unpleasant but simply lacked masculine appeal; and this impression of a lack unleashed streams of troubling pictures in my imagination. These pictures were and still are full of previously registered elements. I saw my mother going out with other men, mostly friends or colleagues of my father; I have a memory of her hastily writing the English words "I love you" on a postcard and drawing a red heart around them; and I suffered through entire nightmares of larger scenes that I had never actually experienced, like my father being laughed at by colleagues, humiliated by the head of the department under whom he worked as a doctor, or failing to score on a penalty shot in the weekend soccer matches that he so enjoyed. What was the form of these chains of impressions in my imaginary, and how were they connected to the omnipresent memory of my father's voice? Those impressions could unfold in dynamic streams and associations that never came together in an imagined and perhaps even truthful story. Mostly, however, they were present as a synthetic ensemble, as a potential of unstable simultaneity, as a substance of content, with the tone of my father's voice being the one focal reference to which all elements were connected. It was a tone both internally complex and dense. As I dreaded this tone and the imaginary ensemble it brought together as a permanent irritating threat, I tried my best to keep it at a distance without ever managing.

More perhaps than other sensual modalities and their intentional objects, tones of individual voices have the capacity of functioning as catalysts that join various elements from our imaginary and our memory. Such ensembles with an individual tone at their center can play different and by no means always painful roles. Some famous voices from the past, obviously voices from the time of sound recording, do function for me as condensations of historical periods and of their imagined atmospheres: the voice, for example, of the incomparable opera tenor Enrico Caruso from the early twentieth century, the voice of the tango singer Carlos Gardel from the glorious 1920s and 30s in Buenos Aires, the post–World War II voice of Edith Piaf, or the voice of Elvis Presley from the American 1960s. They all make present historical moments in their multiple dimensions, as if they had absorbed much of what those moments substantially were.

Is it possible, however, to think of voices and the effects that they trigger functioning as condensing catalysts in our memory, rather than independently of their individual sounds, and that we only retrospectively associate such elements with their actual tones? If some of Piaf's songs—almost too directly—quote motifs of French existentialism (*"Non, je ne regrette rien"*), they also remind me of more dramatic times in their history—together with black-and-white photographs of Paris, with the famous faces of post-war philosophers, with plaques commemorating victims of the German occupation in the streets of Paris, with *la Résistance*, and even—by visual association through a specifically shaped bottle and its label—with the taste of Pernod that I pretended to love.

Ultimately, there is not much new, let alone subtle or insight-producing, in such ensembles. They hold and activate elements that have long been present in my memory, and yet Edith Piaf's voice or the voices of Elvis Presley, Carlos Gardel, and Enrico Caruso give me a connection to their different pasts with an intensity and vivacity that far transcends even the most sophisticated writings of historians. What exactly are voices doing in such cases? My answer again relies on the connection of acoustic perception with visual and tactile impressions in our imaginary. Carlos Gardel's voice invokes pictures of his face and of certain historical sites that I have seen in Buenos Aires, above all some of my favorite soccer stadiums whose architectural shapes date back to the peak of Argentinian culture around 1930. At the same time, as a recorded tactile impression and thus as an impact on my body, Gardel's voice also lends a space to these images in my memory and thus a suggestion of experiencing them in their three-dimensional substance. Recorded voices from the past thus make me feel for a moment that I can inhabit Caruso's Naples and Caruso's New York, Gardel's Buenos Aires and Gardel's Montevideo, Piaf's Paris, and Elvis Presley's Memphis and Las Vegas.

Such full-body effects—produced by the interplay between our perception of voices and the activity of the imaginary triggered by them—can be compared to what sometimes occurs when we hear recited poetry, to the "conjuring up" or making palpable some of the contents that it articulates. Whoever likes to listen to poems or enjoys reading them aloud knows the sense of being physically present in the spaces that they evoke and sharing these spaces with the characters whom they mention. It emerges from the status of prosody, from poetic form or poetic language, as a solution to the problem of how time objects can have a form. As phenomena existing in permanent change, time objects seem incompatible at first glance with our expectation that forms are stable relations between self-reference (for example, a circle pointing to itself) and outside reference (a circle setting itself apart from the world that surrounds it). Rhythm as repetition is indeed prosody's practical way of handling the problem. For while poems proceed in perpetual change on the different levels of language and voice articulation, the structures in which these changes occur repeat themselves. This very repetition suspends the usual effects of time—in processing from a past to a future that is different from it. For the future of a moment in a poem will instead be similar and indeed structurally identical to its past. This is why the recitation of a poem, thanks to rhythm, can exist and remain within its own present, can set itself apart from the running time outside of itself, and can thus also overcome the tension between acoustic perception as bound to time and the synthetic projections of our imagination.[8]

In other words and speaking metonymically, recited poems give the imaginary the stillstand—the space indeed—that it requires as a synthetic projection of our mind. Now as a type of communication based on the repetitions of rhythm instead of being based on permanent change, the recitation of poetry also lowers attention level both for those who recite and for those who listen. Under the condition of lower attention, however, and within their own rhythmic present or space, poems seem to often allow the visual and the tactile modality of our imaginary to enter a fusion where what we believe to see also seems to become palpable. On such a basis poems and songs are particularly strong in inhabiting the worlds of the past to which they belong and in sharing that past as an impression of space with the things and bodies that they evoke.

Being the most salient cultural product of the intersection between voices and our imagination, it is no surprise that the conjuring up effect of recited poetry can never be fully secured or controlled. Independently of the poem's or the recitation's quality, its effect of three-dimensionality sometimes overwhelms us with the liveliness of physical power—and remains mute at other occasions. What we have called the liveliness of imagination triggered by voices may above all consist of that three-dimensionality. Due to their attachment by association to the different sensory modalities of the imaginary, voices can also function in our memory as a focal point that brings together unruly ensembles from the substance of content. The core, however, the most typical structure of imagination triggered by voices lies in the dynamic coexistence between visual and tactile impressions. It permeates all dimensions of our life, unnoticed normally, until it gets activated from outside and provokes long-term pain or intense momentary joy.

Conceptually speaking, the step from voices triggering imagination to willful acts of imagining voices may look like a simple inversion, but the phenomena covered by both topics confront us with profoundly different forms of behavior and their related intellectual problems. I have pointed to the asymmetry between the dynamic and highly centrifugal impact that the perception of voices can have on our minds, and on the other side to the difficulty, if not the resistance, that we often experience when we want to hear voices by activating the acoustic modality of our imagination. Trying to remember the sound of voices that we have heard in the past is the most frequent form of this exercise, if we consider memories as a large dimension within our imaginary.

In general, memories of persons whom we have met and with whom we have interacted in the past will not appear incomplete or lacking if they come without individual sound impressions. We can quite literally remember what somebody said without hearing a specific voice in our mind. If there are any people at all whom we always remember with the sound of their voice, their number must be small. The one obvious threshold for active voice imagining instead lies between those protagonists of our past whose voices we can evoke if we want to do so and those whose voices always remain soundless, despite our strongest efforts. For me at least, this difference is unambiguous and indeed related to the (sometimes treacherous) impression of being able to copy voices whose sounds I hear. If such a sound comes back in my mind, it normally does not have the primary form of a time object but, probably due to the predominantly synthetic functioning of the imaginary, the form of an internally complex tone, of a tone simultaneously containing different sound elements belonging to an individual voice and of a potential for actual speech. As I said, these synthetic impressions often include an urge to redeem them with an articulation of my own voice. At the same time, such complex voice tones are surrounded by memories in different sensory modalities.

Can we identify any criteria that allow us to distinguish and to predict those voices whose sounds we are able to activate under any circumstances? Instead of one overarching answer, my self-observation yields some criteria that depend on different situational circumstances. Above all, I am inclined to remember the sound of voices infused by specific dialects or idiolects, that is by levels of vocal expression that, as I mentioned before, do not fully belong to the range of individual sound qualities. Whenever I think of my late German friend Karl Heinz Bohrer, I hear the upbeat and slightly singing sound of his Cologne accent, dominant even when he tried to speak in foreign languages. Josef Fick, the most inspiring teacher of my gymnasium years, had come back from a one-year exchange visit in Philadelphia with what my classmates and I interpreted as an American accent in his otherwise southern-sounding German, and this tone has become inseparable from my memories of him.

Due to my father's voice, I have a special sensitivity to female tones when men are speaking. Niklas Luhmann, the most provocative German thinker in the humanities and social sciences at the end of the twentieth century, reminded me so much of my father in this sense that I had to habitually isolate his philosophical points from streams of imagination coming from earlier existential stages. What most decidedly strengthens my vocal imagination and memory, by contrast, are the voices of some mentors and friends who accompanied my professional career with understanding and care. I think of them in strong spatial connotations that probably emerge from the link between acoustic and tactile modalities in the imagination. Jean-François Lyotard often becomes present as if he were sitting and speaking in front of me; I hear the warm voice of Hans-Georg Gadamer suggesting the setting and the sociability of a conversation; and whenever the beautifully deep voice of Henry Louis Gates Jr. comes mind, whom I haven't seen in person in decades, I immediately feel like asking him questions about the African American authors he knows so well.

There are surprisingly few other voices whose sounds my imagination manages to activate. The uncanny nasal tone of my great-uncle Franz and the discourse about the freedom he had lost in Siberian captivity still haunts me. I occasionally hear the voice of my teenage girlfriend Claudia in my imagination, with faded promises of erotic adventures that never happened. But no general or individually specific reasons for such lively and mildly obsessive voice memories come to the fore. Of these rare voice memories, most of them have meanwhile survived the persons to whom they belonged, and only a few are grounded in more recent encounters.

What impresses me more than the scattered voices alive in my memory is the stubborn resistance with which my imagination refuses to provide sounds for some of the persons who truly mattered to me. I indeed never hear my mother's voice although, paradoxically, I do have concepts to describe it. I somehow abstractly remember the southwestern German accent of my main academic advisor, the intonation of Wolfgang Iser (a much-admired literary theorist who had been born close to Leipzig), or the Bavarian smoothness in the words of Brigitte Schlieben-Lange from whom I learned so much about the history of Romance languages before her untimely death. But I am as unsuccessful in filling in the discourses I remember with sounds as I am in my efforts to hear the voices of Hilde and Edi, my beloved parents-in-law, who died almost twenty years ago. At some point, I decided to overcome similar frustrations by trying to train my capacity of voice imagining—only to soon give in to the insight that it eludes our agency.

Fiction writers often struggle with similar limitations. Even among those authors who manage to evoke non-existing worlds and their characters with powerful details, we hardly ever find voice descriptions that focus on impressions of sound. While the famous scene of Emma and Charles Bovary's visit to the opera in Rouen is built around the appearance of different singers on the stage, Gustave Flaubert does not give the reader any suggestion about the individual tones of their voices. He characterizes the arias they perform with the abstract terminology of musical scores, moves on to barely mention the "beautiful organ" of Edgar Lagardy, the audience's favorite baritone, and then concentrates on the intense feelings that the singers' voices evoke in Madame Bovary's imagination, without describing the sounds his heroine was supposed to actually hear:

> She was filling her heart with these melodious lamentations that were drawn to the accompaniment of the double-basses, like the cries of the

drowning in the tumult of a tempest. She recognized all the intoxication and the anguish that had almost killed her. The voice of the prima donna seemed to her to be but the echoes of her conscience, and this illusion that charmed her as some actual thing in her own life.

It appears to be easier—and more conventional—for fiction to characterize voices of conscience than to imagine and to evoke the voices of individual characters.

Although Marcel's Proust's *In Search of Lost Time* displays a wide range of voices remembered by the narrator, the novel only seldom focuses on their tones. In those famous scenes from the narrator's childhood where his mother is reading literary texts to him, the descriptions of her voice remain on the level of generic concepts referring to her pedagogical intentions rather than letting us imagine what she might have sounded like:

> [S]he supplied all the natural tenderness, all the lavish sweetness which they demanded to sentences which seemed to have been composed for her voice and which were all, so to speak, within the compass of her sensibility. She found, to tackle them in the required tone, the warmth of feeling which pre-existed and dictated them, but which is not to be found in the words themselves.

The entire novel only offers one exception, and it occurs when the narrator thinks about the reasons of his fascination with Albertine:[9]

> Albertine kept her head motionless and her nostrils pinched, and scarcely moved her lips. The result of this was a drawing, nasal sound, into the composition of which there entered perhaps a provincial heredity, a juvenile affectation of British phlegm, the teaching of a foreign governess and a congestive hypertrophy of the mucus of the nose.

We know that the details in this passage go back to Proust's memory of being a young man—and it must have been a memory in the acoustic memory's full unfolding. By contrast, it will forever remain unclear whether and, if so, how he heard the voice of his mother. Not even Marcel Proust controlled the ways his imagination presented voices.

If will and agency can never fully capture voices in the imaginary, as we have just discussed, what psychologists call auditory hallucinations are voices and other acoustic impressions that are supposedly completely independent of will and agency. These auditory hallucinations are beyond our control, not just subject to our limited control. Like those forms of the imaginary that voices can activate by association, hallucinations exist in all sensory modalities, but unlike those activated in the imagination, the auditory modality clearly dominates among hallucinations, with voice hallucinations related to language accounting for most of them. The question of why hallucinations are above all acoustic—voice- and language-related—has never been convincingly answered.

Everyday language further associates auditory hallucinations with states of psychiatric pathology. While advanced debates about the notions in question may project a more complex picture, it appears sufficient to assume that persons diagnosed with schizophrenia or paranoia normally hear voices in their mind that they cannot escape and from which they suffer. Based on our previous conceptual work, there is reason to insist on two differentiations. In the first place, not all auditory hallucinations should be subsumed under the range of pathologies, and second, as phenomena they are closer to voices in the imaginary than we generally believe. Regarding the content of these voices, it is indeed difficult to distinguish between hallucinations and the imaginary: both come in all sensory modalities, both shift between states of substance without internal and external form and states of form and articulation, and both are specifically close to functions of the human body. As for their origin, we cannot exclude that voices heard in states of schizophrenia or paranoia derive from memories of real voices, as it is typically the case with voices in our imaginary. Finally, both auditory hallucinations and voices in the imaginary challenge agency. Psychiatric therapies and certain religious practices try to mitigate the apparent absoluteness of auditory hallucinations, and at the same time we have seen how personal practices are coping, often unsuccessfully, with equivalent effects emerging from the interplay between voices and imagination.

It is not my intention here to fully blur the difference between auditory hallucinations and voices in the imaginary. But by showing that they are closer to each other than we normally presuppose, we gain an argument against the unconditional subsumption of auditory hallucinations belonging to the category of pathology. The phenomena that we will deal with in the following chapter—for example, as voices of transcendence or voices of gods and also the voice of conscience—largely correspond to the concept of auditory hallucination, without being pathological. Once we have established such an epistemological place for certain voices in the imaginary that are independent of the human will, we can try to understand their specific status and function within cultural history. This precisely is the task that the American scholar Julian Jaynes took up in his highly speculative, eccentric, and therefore inspiring book *The Origin of Consciousness in the Breakdown of the Bicameral Mind*.[10]

Instead of looking for a possible grounding in the details of contemporary brain research, Jaynes started out with a blunt statement of certainty about the existence of hallucinations independently of cultural environment: "Hallucinations must have some innate structure in the nervous system underlying them. We can see this clearly by studying the matter in those who have been profoundly deaf since birth or very early childhood." From this background and only focusing on auditory hallucinations, he moves on to two positions that connect with and further develop some of our previous analyses and reflections in this chapter. Confirming the observation that neither imaginations unleashed by the perception of voices nor attempts to imagine voices can be fully brought under the power of the human will, Jaynes highlights the role of "sound as the least controllable of all sense modalities," and concludes that, for this very reason, voice as a medium of language became decisive for human evolution. Insisting on the specific features of sound and voice in comparison to the other sensory modalities, Jaynes then articulates a further hypothesis that condenses some of our impressions about the functions of voices and also implicitly suggests why hallucinations are predominately sound-related. Mediums of sound, according to him, have a particular authority, an intuition that he illustrates in reference to the voices of gods and to the voices of schizophrenia, "more real to the patients than the doctor's voice." If believers feel that gods reach them by voices above all, it may reflect a human desire for their messages to be binding.

Uncontrollability and authority as complementary core qualities of the voice turn into the leitmotif of a daring speculation about the evolution of human consciousness. In an admittedly radical reading of the *Iliad*, Jaynes sets apart the Greek and the Trojan warriors who exclusively act from the gods who exclusively speak, and he interprets this separation and simultaneity as an early "bicameral" form of the human mind, describing. consciousness as the subsequent stage of an intersection between the two sides of acting and speaking in one system. It is of course pointless to discuss this train of thought within the standards of scientific or at least historical realism. The intellectual value of Jaynes's book lies in the experimental configurations of concepts that it encourages us to take seriously. As for the different types of tensions between voices, the imaginary, and agency that we have identified, we have a reason to play with the idea that sound and voice, as both the least controllable and the most authoritative of all sense modalities, became crucial for the emergence of consciousness as the site of human will. We could indeed go so far to conceive of the will and of agency as an intersection of the voice's uncontrollable energy with its controlling authority.

Notions such as agency, authority, energy, or will do converge in bringing up the question, inevitable for present-day debates among academic humanists, about the relation between power and different forms of voice performance. Departing from the near infinity of far-reaching and indeed metonymical definitions that this concentration has produced, I am inclined to favor a meaning more focused on the bodily dimension of existence and to thereby emphasize the grounding of power in violence understood as a strictly physical process. If we call violence any behavior searching to occupy spaces with bodies against the resistance of other bodies, including individual acts of cruelty like rape or killing, then it becomes plausible to refer to power as a potential of violence—and not as a part of violence that actually happens.

Seen from this angle, we can say that voice performance in its dependence on the use of body organs and, on the other hand, power as a mere potential for violence belong to ontologically separated spheres of life. Our question thus shifts from power to possible connections between voices and violence on the level of physical existence—without arriving at any clear-cut observations or theses. As with most other types of aggressive behavior, acts of violence go frequently (but not necessarily) along with vocal sound production— and humans share this habit with most other mammals. Fight songs in team sports or the singing of military music belong to this culturally developed form. With vocal performance and violence thus being inevitably and yet non-specifically related inside the materiality of human existence, the more interesting cases of their convergence may be those, paradoxically, where vocal effects become deliberately excluded from the execution of violence. In several speeches that he gave after the formal decision about the extermination of Jews at the Wannsee Conference in January 1942, Heinrich Himmler mentioned his concern regarding the "decency" (*Anständigkeit*) of his SS officers being in the presence of their own acts of violence and the resulting mountains of murdered bodies. The solution he alluded to was silence, with the probable implication that, by refraining from words, the SS would preserve their "decency" and depersonalize the operation of industrialized killing, thereby increasing the horror among possible victims and witnesses.

Himmler's strangely vague association leads us back from the execution of violence to the phenomenon and concept of power. Power may have its most devastating impact if it remains as the mere awareness of a potential, without any transition into the real semantic or physical effects of vocal performance. While it would be too optimistic to attribute to vocal performance effects that undermine the control and pain inflicted by power, the perception of voices cannot help triggering individual impulses in our imagination, impulses that may escape the reach of other people's will to power.

In this very sense, due to the interference of imagination, the relation between voice performance and power resembles the different aspects under which voice can challenge agency. With "agency" I am referring to the human capacity of investing individual and collective forms of behavior with the intention and the effect of giving reality to ideas that we have of future situations, however large or small these ideas may be. Different challenges of agency in this sense have been the vanishing point of our attempts to think through three different forms of the interplay between voices and imagination in this chapter. We have seen how difficult it can be to control processes in the imaginary triggered by the perception of voices, to conjure up the sound of individual voices in the imaginary, and to cope with the impact of voices from auditory hallucinations. These are all types of behavior on the verge of agency. Given the difference, however, not to mention the discontinuity between the phenomena dealt with in the preceding sections, it is far from obvious why exactly each of the three connections ended up confronting us with challenges of agency.

The most elementary reason for this convergence, I believe, results from specific ambiguities that both voice and imagination have in relation to agency, from ambiguities also that produce remarkable degrees of complexity in their interaction and their differences. As media for the articulation of propositional content, voices are subject to human agency, but our intentional behavior has hardly any impact on the effects produced by their individual tones. Likewise, imagining can well be conceived as an intentional act of producing determinate sensory effects in our mind although the success and the consequences of such acts largely evade our agency. Translated into everyday language: activating forms of interplay between sounds of voices and the imaginary often create considerable confusion.

As a second approach for comparing and understanding the different relations among voices, imagination, and agency, I use the question, cultivated in the German tradition of philosophical anthropology, about advantages and disadvantages to which such structures of phenomena may have been connected in different stages of human evolution. When we hear the sounds of voices coming from bodies that we cannot see, it produces a peculiar energy and intensity in the imaginary, which may go back to the need of early humans, living without established institutions, to protect themselves against invisible dangers. It is plausible to assume that the interplay between voices perceived and the imagination functioned as an efficient warning system that we have inherited and can now, in the absence of its original function, enjoy or try to keep silent.

By contrast, I do not see a similar evolutionary context for the difficulty required to conjure up the sounds of individual voices in our imaginary. While it surely is a pleasure to hear a beloved voice in our imagination and while the distinctive talent of composers may indeed consist of the capacity to imagine the performance of a symphony or of an aria that they have created, very little hinges upon such capacities for the survival or for the progress of humankind. This may account for the sometimes frustrating and altogether astonishing realization that the powers of our imagination remain limited when it comes to evoking individual voices.

The non-pathological forms of auditory hallucinations—that is, voices of gods and the voice of conscience—bring up a different context that is more historical than evolutionary. There are certainly abundant theories about the functions of religion in early stages of humankind. By contrast and compared to predominant expectations about the disappearance of gods in the Western process of modernity, I find it remarkable how many people, in our otherwise thoroughly secular present, continue to distinctly hear divine voices as voices of authority and occasionally as voices of personal support. It must be an existential rather than evolutionary longing for a force beyond agency that has kept them alive.

Julian Jaynes's speculation about the evolution of consciousness offers a third possibility for thinking about voices, imagination, and the limits of agency. Taking up his idea about the transition of the authoritative voice of transcendence from an imaginary horizon into the human mind as the decisive step in the formation of consciousness, we can extrapolate that the—former—voice of transcendence must have subsequently covered the—new—role and function of volition as the core of agency: as the power and the energy necessary for the transubstantiation of visions (or motivations) into reality. In addition to the association between the authority of a transcendental voice and the energy of volition, Jaynes had also described sounds and voices as the "least controllable" sensory modality in the imaginary.

Consequently, the relation between agency and imagined voices appears as a relation between the former transcendental voices turned into volition and the voices present in the imaginary remaining unruly. One could characterize this structure of tension between the two opposite sides of one phenomenon—its directed energy and its unruliness—as a paradox or as a dialectic relation inherent to the lives of imagined voices (if the concept of dialectic ever yielded more clarity than confusion). One way or the other, tension as paradox or dialectic, trying to describe the different, mutually enhancing and mutually restraining relations between voices and the imaginary has proven to be an intellectually productive dwelling on the verge of agency.

———— SIX

Voices with Neutral Perfection
THE ADDRESS OF
TRANSCENDENTAL AUTHORITY

BY NO MEANS IS MOSES the first human to whom the God of the Old Testament[1] speaks, but it is only with their encounter in Exodus 3: 1 that the ontological discontinuity, setting apart the divine voice from human perception, begins to become a problem and an occasional topic for the text. Born from Jewish ancestors in exile and raised under the protection of the pharaoh's daughter, Moses had killed an Egyptian whom he saw "beating a Hebrew" and then fled to the land of the Midianites, remote relatives of Israel, where he married a daughter of the priest Jethro. This existence far away from his people of origin may explain why God finds it necessary to attract the attention of Moses with a specific approach, as the latter is keeping the cattle of his father-in-law near the mountain that will become Israel's holy mountain Sinai.

Instead of addressing Moses directly, God has an angel silently appear "to him in a flame of fire out of a bush; he looked, and the bush was blazing, yet it was not consumed." Once God can be sure that Moses concentrates on this "great sight," he assumes the angel's place and uses his own voice to call his creature's name "out of the bush, 'Moses, Moses!' And he said: 'Here I am.'" Then God warns

Moses not to come any closer, orders him to take off his sandals because he is standing on holy ground, and finally identifies himself: "I am the God of your father, the God of Abraham, the God of Isaac, and the God of Jacob." Knowing with irrefutable certainty who is in front of him, Moses feels afraid and hides his face. All these steps determining the conditions for the divine voice to be heard by human ears are preliminary to an exchange of words in which God seeks to commission Moses with leading the people of Israel out of Egyptian captivity, whereas Moses tries to withdraw from the assignment by referring to his lack of "eloquence." Strangely, given the manifest hierarchy established between him and Moses, God's voice fails to be immediately efficient.

Not only from the scriptures of Judaism and Christianity are we familiar with scenes where gods use their voices, more than any other tool of communication, to interact with humans, and we expect these voices to sound perfect in any imaginable dimension. There are, for example, sixteen canonized qualities attributed to the voice of Brahma, the main god of Hinduism, from "fluent, intelligent, sweet" to "audible, continuous, and deep," while a plethora of sixty adjectives is associated with the Buddha's voice. Such broad horizons of concepts quite regularly add up to convey an initial impression of superior authority to the speeches of gods. The ancient Greek tradition, by contrast, tells us less about the voices of individual deities (only Zeus sounds mostly "thunderous") but condenses symbolisms of signs and sounds in the Muses as goddesses of inspiration. Among them, Calliope stands out as an allegory of the singing voice, described by Dante in the first canto of "Paradiso" from *The Divine Comedy as* "striking a higher key, / Accompanying her song with that sweet air." Aoede, another, less frequently mentioned Muse also associated with voice and singing, is described in mythology as a deity comprised of her vocal organs.

Such variations of perfection and completeness give to our impression of divine voices a flair of neutrality. As they are supposed to possess all thinkable positive qualities, they lack individuality and can thus never exhibit through their sound what we have called "a grain." And as they do not have a grain, divine voices do not correspond to our description of the human voice as having "lives" and as experiencing a "knot" where the meanings articulated interfere with the effects of the imaginary triggered by an individual sound. From a logical standpoint, divine voices are quite differently supposed to combine the function of meaning articulation with an absolute status of authority, efficiency, and agency inaccessible to humans. If, however, we generally understand the voice to be a human voice and this concept is not compatible with our elementary ideas about transcendental beings and their voices, then why does the association between gods and voices occur so very frequently? This question is the focus of this chapter.

An immediate answer seems to come from the previous chapter where, encouraged by Julian Jaynes and his book on the bicameral mind, we attributed a superiority and liveliness among the senses to the human voice and to hearing. But we interpreted such qualities as emerging from the capacity of voices to challenge human agency and control, a capacity grounded in the inspirational impact of individual forms of sound—and thus not pertaining to the imagination of divine voices. To summarize, we have shown that there is a compelling explanation for the connection that we so often make between deities and voices, *but* this explanation falls apart when we consider that it applies exclusively to human voices.

It is precisely this difficulty that gives the voices of transcendence an intellectually promising status as it highlights the gap between the discourses with which we try to describe them and our knowledge of the human voice. I analyze several historical cases for the evocation of transcendental voices because I believe that the topic could potentially lead us to insights about the functions of human voices that we have not recognized so far and that we may not be able to see through any different route. In other words, I deal with a predominantly religious repertoire of texts, motifs, and phenomena with the expectation of bringing to the fore some knowledge of clearly secular value. My interpretations of discourses and narratives about voices of transcendence thus gauge their success and failure, their efficiency, and their problems in reaching humans from the secular angle of cultural phenomenology—under the premise that what we call "gods" can be considered products of the human imagination fulfilling certain social and psychic functions—while I have no vested interest in denying the existence of transcendent realities.

In this sense, the concept of transcendental authority from the chapter title doesn't only refer to the cultural phenomena we refer to as gods and associate with different degrees of superiority over humans in everyday language. It also includes forms of human behavior that pretend, and that many of us believe to be, inspired by divine influence, such as the voices of prophets or "speaking in tongues." Finally, the frequently used expression "voice of conscience" makes me realize that what we call conscience structurally participates in the status of transcendence. We normally "hear" conscience as a movement in our mind that transcends individual agency or volition—and therefore quite often, although not necessarily, gets identified as a divine intervention.

The order in which I deal with voices attributed to gods, to humans under divine inspiration, and to conscience as a function of independence within the human mind is chronological on an elementary level. I begin with commentaries on several passages from the Old Testament and try to develop an understanding of the astonishingly precarious status that they give to the authority of God's voice and its reach. For the gospel and for the Christian tradition, I again highlight the modality of incarnation as a premise of thought and behavior that can allow for the successful delegation of powers associated with divine voices to human voices. We then focus on Islam as the one monotheistic religion whose conception of God consequently avoids speaking functions or vocal articulations and thereby proves that the association of gods with voices is not a general theological necessity. My concluding reflections are about the "voice of conscience" as a case for the connection between transcendence and voice in a predominantly secular present, a case that—by getting us closer to a general understanding of the reasons for the frequent association between transcendence and voices—can expand our thinking about voices in the everyday.

God's creation of the world, with which the Old Testament begins in a both monumental and startling gesture, does not occur as a creation out of nothingness. The earth is already there as "a formless void," and "darkness covered the void" to which God gives form. If we follow the text sentence by sentence, we see that, at least during the first few days of creation, God does not use his hands but his voice—although the text does not explicitly use this word yet: "Then God said, 'let there be light'; and there was light." Without any association to a specific sound, God's voice exerts unconditional power over the formless void and over the darkness.

For the second day, it is possible to read God's speech as an announcement of his plan because the sentence "Let there be a dome in the midst of the waters, and let it separate the waters from the waters" is followed by the explicit reference to a forming activity: "So God made the dome and separated the waters that were under the dome from the waters that were above the dome." After God calls the dome "sky," another behavior that we imagine as voice-related, the text of Genesis on the third day returns to the pattern of an immediate efficiency of God's voice, an efficiency over matter that we refer to as "magical" in the languages of modernity: "And God said, 'Let the waters under the sky be gathered together into one place, and let the dry land appear.' And it was so."

Only the creation of humankind "in God's image, according to God's likeness" on the seventh day clearly departs from this model. Rather than confirming the fulfillment of his will, the declaration of God's plan for the creation and for the cosmological role of humans is followed by the words: "So God created humankind in his image" and later by the more detailed descriptions of making the "man from the dust of the ground" and the woman from "the rib that the Lord God had taken from the man." Already before the final stage of his work, however, resulting in the woman's appearance, God had "commanded the man," in words directly spoken to him, that he might "freely eat of every tree" in his garden of Eden, but that "of the tree of the knowledge of good and evil you shall not eat, for in the day that you eat of it you will die."

It is tempting to read the subsequent narrative of the Fall as a story about the limits of the power of God's voice in its relation to humans. Unlike the neutrality of its divine perfection, the first verse of Genesis 3 suggests a seductiveness in the words of the serpent by calling it "more crafty than any other animal that God had made." In addition, we can identify at least a partial truth in the serpent's voice when, directed to the woman, it contradicts God's warning that man will die if he eats from the tree of knowledge: "You will not die for God knows that when you eat of it your eyes will be opened, and you will be like God." Had God's voice lied to his creatures by warning them against their curiosity with an overstatement of its potential consequences—as so many human parents do? After all, instead of dying from eating the fruit of the tree, the eyes of the man and the woman indeed "were opened, and they knew that they were naked." The point about the truth value and the obvious failure of God's warning words may be of small importance theologically or mythologically, but they still constitute a contrast against which we recognize a different function of God's speech when a specific word for "voice" appears for the first time.

While the woman and the man are busy sewing "fig leaves together and making loincloths for themselves" to cover their now-embarrassing nakedness, they "heard the sound of the Lord God walking in the garden at the time of the evening breeze, and the man and his wife hid themselves from the presence of the Lord God among the trees of the garden." But they do not manage to withdraw from their Creator. When God calls the man "and said to him, 'Where are you?' He said, 'I heard the sound of you in the garden, and I was afraid, because I was naked.'" God no longer speaks neutrally here, without any individual features.

Behind the substantive "sound" that comes up twice in the verses that I am quoting from an English translation of Genesis,[2] stands for the first time the Hebrew word *kol*, today meaning both "voice" and "sound"—which explains why some other English translations use "voice" instead of "sound" in the passages where Adam refers to his perception of God.[3] With the emergence of the word *kol* and its specific semantics, God's voice acquires a palpable physical quality, and this palpable physical quality accounts for the man and woman's inability to hide from him. We can thus state that, due to the occurrence of the Hebrew word for "voice" with its particular meaning, God's speech gains greater power within the narrative. By contrast, God seems to play a different, less imposing role of divinity in those scenes of Genesis that merely refer to him as "speaking" without explicitly mentioning his voice. I further pursue this difference because it seems to account for a differentiated assessment of the success and failure attributed to God's voice in the Old Testament.

From Genesis 3: 9, we advance in the narrative and return to God's commission for Moses in Exodus 3: 7 and following, to lead his people out of the Egyptian exile. After "four hundred thirty years" of captivity ending with several encounters between Moses and the pharaoh, whom, for all of the divine support at hand, Moses cannot persuade to let the Israelites go, God now strikes "down all the firstborn in the land of Egypt" and thus facilitates the exit of "about six hundred thousand men, besides children." In three months of journey, they arrive at "the wilderness of Sinai" where God had already talked to Moses and where Moses now goes "up to God." Here the most substantial part of the Old Testament for Judaism as an institution begins with the Creator's reminder to Moses of what he "did to the Egyptians" and above all with the promise that "if you obey My voice and keep My covenant, you shall be My treasured possession out of all the people. Indeed, the whole earth is Mine, but you shall be for Me a priestly kingdom and a holy nation. These are the words that you shall speak to the Israelites."

From this point on Moses will act as the mediator of God's voice. Throughout his subsequent visits to the mountain, however, the asymmetry between God and him continues to be manifest, while it progressively turns from a fear-inspiring hierarchy into the emerging security of a ritual. Part of the ritual is a spatial distance established by the God of "thunder and lightning," between his voice and his people, a distance that the Israelites desire to keep as they say to Moses: "You speak to us, and we will listen; but do not let God speak to us, or we will die."

When Moses ascends to the mountain for the second time, accompanied only by his brother Aaron, God pronounces "all the words" of the commandments and of the covenant's rules to him in the neutral gesture of supreme authority, after identifying himself again: "I am the Lord your God, you shall have no other Gods before Me." And while Moses tells "the people" and writes "down all the words of the Lord," God calls him again with a new announcement: "Come up to Me on the mountain, and wait there; and I will give you the tablets of stone, with the law and the commandments, which I have written for their instruction" (Exodus 24: 12). Why are these tablets required, in addition to the power of God's voice and with Moses as both a speaking and writing mediator?

After multiple further instructions for the Israelites, we read: "When God finished speaking with Moses on Mount Sinai, He gave him the tablets of the covenant, tablets of stone, written with the finger of God" (Exodus 31: 18). The narrative now takes a dramatic turn, but there are only scant proposals to help us interpret this development. Carrying the "two tablets that were written on both sides, written on the front and on the back," Moses first hears and then sees his people in their "camp," dancing around a "calf," and his "anger burned hot, and he threw the tablets from his hands and broke them at the foot of the mountain. He took the calf that they had made, burned it with fire, ground it to powder, scattered it on the water, and made the Israelites drink it" (Exodus 32: 19–20).

God's voice has failed to prevent his people from "running wild" for the calf, instead of observing the covenant that both he and Moses had fixed in writing. And although God's voice did not have sufficient power, Moses, who loses control as he angrily breaks the tablets, could have compensated for the failure of God's voice. Neither God's voice alone nor the tablets alone was sufficiently strong to keep the covenant, which explains why, after imposing several punishments on the Israelites, Moses dares to ask God to give them another chance, as we would say today, and why God concedes to "do the very thing" that Moses, as a now-confirmed mediator, proposes: "for you have found favor in My sight and I know you by name." But this time God chooses a different strategy. Instead of handing the commandments to Moses, he instructs him to cut "two tablets of stones like the former ones" and to then inscribe them. God also orders that the new tablets will rest "in the ark that" Moses "had made" (Deuteronomy 10: 5) and that they shall travel further with God's people and end up in his temple at Jerusalem.

Ultimately, the interaction of God and Moses, with its alternation between God's voice and the tablets "inscribed by His finger," helps us understand why Judaism has existed throughout the centuries "in the dualism of a written text and its oral presence through Talmud and Midrash."[4] Even in such complementary dualism, the reach and authority of God's voice will always remain precarious.

Multiple episodes from the Old Testament illustrate this state of the contact between God and different representatives of his people, a state that may surprise observers unfamiliar with the practices of Judaism. We can sense a profound and lasting desire for signs and events that confirm the presence of transcendental power and give clarity to the directions of its orientation. When such messages occur, they sometimes bypass the medium of language. Gideon, a future general who will lead the Israelites to an important victory over the vastly larger army of the Midianites, insists on several proofs from God in order to trust the message that he "will deliver Israel by my hand, as He has said" (Judges 6: 37). Gideon first dares to ask for the miracle of a fleece from wool penetrated by dew that lies on completely dry ground. When on the next morning he "had wrung enough dew from the fleece to fill a bowl with water," he is still not convinced and wants to see a dry fleece on a surface of dew. "God did so that night," and finally Gideon departs with his soldiers for the battle.

Even the sound of God's voice and its explicit announcements occasionally cause confusion. We read that "the word of the Lord was rare" in the days of young Samuel who will later contribute to the foundation of Israel's kingdom. While he was "lying down in the temple of the Lord, where the ark of God was" (Samuel 3: 3), God calls him "Samuel! Samuel!" without identifying himself as God, and

Samuel, "who did not yet know the Lord," believes to have heard the elderly priest Eli "whose eyesight had begun to dim so that he could not see and was lying in his room." Three times Samuel presents himself to Eli, saying, "Here I am, for you called me," only to receive Eli's answer, "I did not call, lie down again." In the end it is Eli who understands "that the Lord was calling the boy" and tells Samuel to respond by saying, "Speak Lord, for your servant is listening." But what Samuel finally hears from God only adds to his insecurity, for God reveals that he is about "to punish Eli's house forever, for the inequity that he knew." Only to the degree that Samuel grows up will he develop sufficient openness for the frequently enigmatic content of God's voice and thus become his "trustworthy prophet."

Not even role of the prophet, however, is exempt from precariousness in the communication between God and Israel. Jeremiah, for example, must use his authority to warn the believers in the name of the Lord against other prophets (Jeremiah 23: 29 ff): "I am against the prophets, says the Lord, who use their own tongues and say, 'Says the Lord.' See, I am against those who prophesy lying dreams, says the Lord, and who tell them and who lead My people astray by their lies and their recklessness."

However, in the middle of so much doubt and such loud polemics in the Old Testament, we discover passages where God speaks in unexpected tones to find the believers' ears and to give authenticity to his voice. When the Prophet Elijah is waiting for a message from God that shall rescue him from the fellow Israelites "who are seeking his life to take it away" (Kings 19: 10 ff), he hears a wind "but the Lord was not in the wind." And after the wind, an earthquake, "but the Lord was not in the earthquake," and then a fire, "but the Lord was not in the fire." Remaining mute God paradoxically articulates himself in "a sound of sheer silence," out of which "came a voice that said 'What are you doing here, Elijah?'" Does God's voice here renounce the objectivity of its physical sound to become more efficient?

More than being the carrier of clear messages and instructions, the voice of God in the Old Testament functions as a reference for our longing for moments of direct address from the side of transcendence. We may associate such longing with an imagination (perhaps still remotely alive in Jewish culture), with a divine voice of irresistible physical immediacy, with a voice that perhaps once existed and has been lost forever. Juxtaposing voice as meaning and voice as sound, the concept of *kol* in the present-day use of Hebrew could be the trace of a "voice-thing": as a substantial, non-dualistic union of meaning and sound—or the projection of a collective yearning for it.[5] This speculation about *kol* as the "voice-thing" may illustrate how the precariousness of its reach, and of its processing that accompanies God's voice in the Old Testament, has energized and still energizes a desire to assign to it an epistemologically exceptional status.

To understand the quite different status that the divine voice developed in Christianity, we need to acknowledge the larger framework of conditions under which the new religion emerged from Judaism. Contemporary scholarship leaves no doubt about the existence of Jesus as a historical figure. Born in the northern region of what today we can refer to as Israel and crucified under the authority of Roman occupation, he most likely was a reform-promoting rabbi whom a group of followers revered as a prophet during his lifetime. The theologically peculiar role of Jesus as "God's son" within the inherently paradoxical Christian conception of trinitarian monotheism must have resulted from the initiative, mainly associated with Saint Paul, of opening up the group of his former disciples and of post-mortem admirers to the non-Jewish "gentiles" of the Roman empire. If they wanted to believe in Jesus Christ as a divine figure essentially independent of Judaism, most of the Jews attracted by his words must have tended to see him as the fulfillment of messianic prophecies from their own religion—the word "Christ" was indeed originally used as a Greek translation for the Hebrew word "Messiah," the "anointed."

While it was thus plausible for the Jews among the followers of Jesus to call him Messiah and a "son" of their god, this status and the concept of a son at the same time became part of the trinitarian and yet monotheistic god that the emerging new theology presented to the gentiles. What decisively contributed to the astonishing resonance that the Trinity found as the logically precarious solution to a mediation problem between two religiously different constituencies was the role given to the concept of incarnation. It allowed Christians to reconcile memories of the historical Jesus with the transcendent position that he had inherited, so to speak, from the god of the Old Testament. And as a problem solution, the notion of the Trinity, made possible by incarnation, became the premise of an innovative way to react to God's voice that, in later institutional contexts, would allow for delegating its efficiency to human voices.

The biographical narratives of the gospel stage the event of Jesus's baptism as an overture for the emergence of the Trinity and incarnation as new and decisive theological notions. While Christian commentaries—due to the contradictory nature of an act of baptism applied to a protagonist who is supposed to be God's son (a criterion of embarrassment)—usually emphasize that this episode must be grounded in a historically existing ritual, the textual reference to the voice of God the Father that it contains attributes a specific role to Jesus early on in the texts of Matthew, Mark, and Luke:

> Now when all the people were baptized, and when Jesus also had been baptized and was praying, the heaven was opened, and the Holy Spirit descended upon him in bodily form like a dove. And a voice came from heaven, 'You are my Son, the Beloved, with whom I am well pleased. (Luke 3: 21–22)

The appearance of a dove as a representation of transcendental authority goes far back in the Mesopotamian and then in the Jewish tradition, but what I find particularly remarkable here is the insistence on the "bodily form" of the dove and the explicit appearance of the word "voice." God the Father's presence has a physical substantiality here that it seldom, if ever, assumes in the Old Testament.

Against this background, the scene referred to as the Transfiguration became crucial for the theological understanding of Jesus as God incarnate. About halfway through the Gospel of Matthew and a few days after the Apostle Peter used the word "Christ" for the first time in reference to his master, Jesus takes "with him Peter and James and his brother John and led them up a high mountain" where he is "transfigured before them" (Matthew 17: 1–2). Both a visual and a social change are taking place: "his face shone like the sun, and his clothes became dazzling white. Suddenly there appeared to them Moses and Elijah, talking with him." As Peter finds "it is good for us to be here," he proposes to give permanence to this situation by making "three dwellings here, one for you, one for Moses, and one for Elijah." But "a voice" interrupts him and repeats "from a bright cloud" what God had said after the baptism of Jesus: "This is my Son, the Beloved; with him I am well pleased; listen to him!" The words "listen to him!" give increased authority to Jesus, and the apostles' reaction to God's voice now reminds us of Moses in the first encounter with the God of the Old Testament: "they fell to the ground and were overcome by fear" (Matthew 17: 6).

Transfiguration, however, turns into incarnation with the subsequent sentences: "Jesus came and touched the apostles saying, 'Get up and do not be afraid.' And when they looked up, they saw no one except Jesus himself alone." The bright cloud from which God had spoken is no longer there. If the apostles now see "no one except Jesus himself alone," this means that his physical presence as a human, manifested by his touch and by his words, has taken over the physical presence of God the Father's voice having referred to him as "my Son, the Beloved." Incarnation thus happens in the very moment when the transfigured human body of Jesus, whom the apostles see "alone," lends its presence as a reference to God the Father's voice. In the Christian reading of the text, Jesus becomes Christ and one with the god of the Old Testament exactly in this passage, which gives to the event of Transfiguration a superior status as the first epiphany of the trinitarian god's preexisting union. We see how the gospel binds the Trinity to incarnation through the voice as a primordial medium of their joint physicality. The individual human body of Jesus gives physical substance to God's voice—without however transforming God's voice into a voice with an individual sound.

Becoming part of the trinitarian god does not fully liberate Jesus from the possibility of human weakness. In the Gospel of John, the chapters about his passion play out this ambiguity of the incarnate Jesus in scenes underlining the confusion that his existence could provoke. As a human being, Jesus is afraid of the bodily suffering whose imminence he anticipates: "'Now my soul is troubled. And what should I say—"Father, save me from this hour"?'" Although Jesus must find the answer to his own question, he asks for a confirmation from the god of whom he is part: "'No, it is for this reason that I have come to this hour. Father, glorify your name.' Then a voice came from heaven, 'I have glorified it, and I will glorify it again'" (John 13: 27 ff). And as the divine voice reacts to the human weakness of Jesus, the crowd "standing around" underestimates it "and said it was thunder. Others said, 'An angel has spoken to him.'"

According to the implied concept of the Trinity, however, a voice that speaks for God the Father cannot possibly address Jesus Christ who is a dimension of the same God. Jesus therefore corrects the crowd: "This voice has come for your sake, not for mine," and adds further words about his future death and about being "lifted up from the earth," only provoking more confusion among those who are familiar with Jewish law: "The crowd answered him, 'We have heard from the law that the Messiah remains forever. How can you say that the Son of Man has to be lifted up? Who is the Son of Man?'" (John 12: 34–35). Jesus no longer answers this question coming from the crowd and changes to a different discursive tonality: "The light is with you for a little longer. Walk while you have the light, so that the darkness may not overtake you."

From here the text of the gospel moves on to emphasize that the unwillingness of the Jews to understand the "many signs" of Jesus and their refusal to "believe in him" only "fulfills the word spoken by the Prophet Isaiah." Knowing that the text of the gospel goes back to a time after the Epistles of Saint Paul with what they took from Judaism, we can interpret the ambiguity in relation to the voice of Jesus that it evokes: the Jews don't believe in Jesus, but the Old Testament anticipated his mission as corresponding to the program of the new religion; the gospel wanted to remain open to Jews without making Judaism a precondition for being Christian.

The final words spoken by Jesus in the gospel again illustrate his human nature. Only here an adjective ("loud") appears to describe the tone of an individual moment in the sound of his voice, and only here the Gospel of Matthew quotes and translates what the historical Jesus is supposed to have said in his native Aramaic: "From noon on, darkness came over the whole land until three in the afternoon. And about three o'clock Jesus cried with a loud voice, 'Eli, Eli, lema sabachthani?' that is, 'My God, my God, why have you forsaken me?'" Perhaps because *Eli* is the Aramaic word for "my God," a new misunderstanding occurs: "When some of the bystanders heard it, they said, 'This man is calling for Elijah.' . . . But the others said, 'Wait, let us see whether Elijah will come to save him'" (Matthew 27: 45 ff). The final sentence referring to the physical life of Jesus again mentions his voice: "Then Jesus cried again with a loud voice and breathed his last. At that moment the curtain on the temple was torn in two, from top to bottom. The earth shook, and rocks were split" (Matthew 27: 50–51).

What truly changes between the passages invoking God's voice in the Old Testament and in the New Testament concerns their theological status rather than their descriptive semantics. In continued expectation of the Messiah, the meaning and the success of messages from the speaking God have never ceased to be precarious for Judaism. By contrast, Christianity—by assigning the role of the Messiah to Jesus and conceiving of his relation to God the Father within the Trinity mediated by incarnation—abandoned the premise of a distance between God and humans and thus attributed to the voice of Jesus an at least theologically unlimited accessibility, transparency, and efficiency. This directness of address also changed the role of humans from searching for an understanding of God to being open to his revelations as a pathway for human life. Although Jesus and his voice still oscillate between incarnate perfection and human weakness in the final passages of the gospel narratives, the Acts of the Apostles allow us to understand how the Christian religion progressively established itself, on the basis of incarnation, as a means of delegating divine power to human voices.

Written in all likelihood by the same author as the Gospel of Luke, the narrative of the Acts of the Apostles begins with a sentence that alludes to a new state of unambiguous clarity in the presence and in the occasional messages of Jesus during the limited time of his incarnate life following the Crucifixion: "After his suffering he presented himself alive to the apostles by many convincing proofs, appearing to them for forty days and speaking about the kingdom of God" (Acts 1: 3 ff). While the disciples still expect Jesus to fulfill the inner-Jewish prophecies related to the figure of the Messiah 9 9 9 ("Lord, is this the time when you will restore the Kingdom of Israel?"), Jesus, in words that contradict neither these prophecies nor the concept of the Trinity, refuses to answer their questions about the immediate future and announces that the "Holy Spirit will come down upon them"; he is lifted up in "a cloud that took him out of their sight as they were watching." While the event of Ascension ends the incarnate presence of Jesus on earth, we see how, according to theological understanding, his voice preserves the force to intervene in human time.

Perhaps as a symptom of uncertainty among the disciples regarding the presence of Jesus, his name does not appear in the account about the holiday of Pentecost and its events, although this passage does function as a fulfillment of his prophecy about the Holy Spirit, made immediately before Ascension. Beginning with signs that have often announced the appearance of God in the Old Testament, the specific symbolism of the Pentecostal scene highlights the impact of the Spirit on the apostles' speaking power:

> And suddenly from heaven there came a sound like the rush of violent wind, and it filled the entire house where they were sitting. Divided tongues, as of fire, appeared among them, and a tongue rested on each of them. All of them were filled with the Holy Spirit and began to speak in other languages, as the Spirit gave them ability. (Acts 2: 2)

In physical absence of the incarnate Jesus, it is now the Holy Spirit, as the third person of the trinitarian god, who gives to the apostles a new linguistic capacity that strictly speaking does not have to manifest itself in the sound of their voices. And yet they insist that they are competent to preach in languages that they have never learned and reject the suspicion of those Jews assembled in Jerusalem who believe that they are "filled with new wine" and thus talk out of an intoxicated mind: "Indeed these are not drunk, as you suppose," says Peter, "for it is only nine o'clock in the morning." But above all, the apostles use their foreign languages exclusively to impress other Jews at this point of the narrative; they continue to interpret the new awe that "came upon everyone, because many wonders and signs were being done by them" (Acts 2: 43) within the framework of Jewish prophecies, and thus never fully and definitively elevate Jesus to a discursive and theological level that unites him with God:

> Jesus of Nazareth, man attested to you by God with deeds of power, wonders, and signs that God did through him among you, as you yourselves know—this man, handed over to you according to the definite plan and foreknowledge of God, you crucified and killed by the hands of those outside the law. But God raised him up, having freed him from death, because it was impossible for him to be held in its power. (Acts 2: 22 ff)

The theologically charged word "voice" and the name of Jesus do not jointly return in the Acts before the conversion of Saul who, as Saint Paul and as a historical figure, will open to the gentiles the inner-Jewish movement around the apostles and their belief in a Messiah. As it happens after Christ's Ascension, the event prefigures and inaugurates the potential of his incarnate voice to become present in other human bodies. Saul appears for the first time in a scene about the Christian martyr Stephen, who professes "Jesus standing at the right hand of God" (Acts 8: 55–56) and therefore gets "dragged out of Jerusalem and stoned, and the witnesses laid their coats at the feet of a young man named Saul. And Saul approved of their killing him."

All of Saul's activities so far have indeed converged in an effort to prevent the new Jewish sect—that thanks to baptism was spreading all over the ancient world—from becoming an independent religion. Then, "breathing threads and murder against the disciples of the Lord" on his way to Damascus from where he wants to bring his enemies "bound to Jerusalem," he is suddenly hit "by a light from heaven that flashed around him" (Acts 9: 3). The verbal address that follows this visual impression in the Old Testament's style of divine epiphanies departs from the tradition. For its impact comes from a voice that specifically embodies God's son and his fate among humans: Saul "fell to the ground and heard a voice saying to him, 'Saul, Saul, why do you persecute me?'" Immediately Saul realizes that this cannot be the Jewish god in whose name he had believed to act, and he asks: "'Who are you, Lord?' The reply came, 'I am Jesus, whom you are persecuting. But get up and enter the city, and you will be told what you are to do'" (Acts 9: 3 ff).

Having quite literally returned to earth with his voice, Jesus holds back its message and its further physical impact on Saul, "who got up from the ground, and though his eyes were open, could see nothing." For the first time now and probably because his bodily presence among humans had come to an end, Jesus will delegate the power of his voice to a human voice, quite plausibly to the voice of a man among his believers:

> Now there was a disciple in Damascus named Ananias. The Lord said to him in a vision: "Ananias." He answered: "Here I am, Lord." The Lord said to him, "Get up and go to the street called Straight, and at the house of Judas look for a man of Tarsus named Saul."

Similar to Moses in Exodus, Ananias first tries to escape this assignment and refers to the "evil" that he knows Saul has done to the "saints in Jerusalem." But when Ananias finally obeys, he frees Saul from blindness by using his own voice and his own hands in the same magical way that until then had been Jesus's privilege:

> Ananias went and entered the house. He laid his hands on Saul and said, "Brother Saul, the Lord Jesus, who appeared to you on your way here, has sent me so that you may regain your sight and be filled with the Holy Spirit." And immediately something like scales fell from his eyes, and his sight was restored. Then he got up and was baptized.

The human touch and the human voice of Ananias had exerted divine power. Although this aspect is seldom mentioned, we can interpret the role of Ananias in Saul's conversion as a foundational anticipation of Christian, more precisely, of Catholic priesthood.

The performative and theological core of this scene lies in its structural analogy with the magical[6] power of transubstantiating bread and wine into the flesh and blood of Jesus to the human voice of a priest, who repeats the words that God's son spoke during the Last Supper. A similar, supposedly real impact belongs to the priest's voice in the moment of absolution at the end of the confession ritual and also to the words used in the act of blessing. Among the sacraments, we can say that the priestly ordination most specifically reenacts the delegation of the voice of Jesus to Ananias, and this delegation relies on incarnation as the condition of human bodies to perform acts of divinity. From a Catholic perspective, the priest's voice thus allows a conjuring up of the material presence and power of the trinitarian god in human time. Returning to our metaphor of the knot of the voice, the physical voice of the incarnate god delegates its conjuring force to the sound of the priest's voice.

This configuration between the divine and a human voice does not exist in the theological and institutional understanding of Protestantism. Among other early modern theologians, Martin Luther interpreted the Eucharist as a ritual in commemoration of the Last Supper—and thus abandoned its function of repeating and making present the original act of transubstantiation. Taking a different stance on the genealogy of delegation that begins with Ananias, the voice of the Protestant pastor becomes a normal human voice again. When Luther, at the 1521 Diet of Worms, tried to justify the new exegesis of the gospel and its theological consequences, he referred to the ultimately secular and individual instance of his "conscience" as "captive to the voice of God"—far from invoking his own voice as a priestly incarnation of divine power. The belief in the possibility of delegating functions of God's voice to a human voice had vanished for him.

Islam is the one monotheistic religion whose texts do not feature a god speaking to humans. As such, I will focus on the notion of its god as a contrast in order to develop further arguments and answers in our search to understand the specific impulse that makes other cultures obsessed with connecting transcendental authorities to voices. From a theological angle, Islam's divergence from Judaism and Christianity has to do with Allah's more pronounced remoteness from the earthly world, a remoteness underlining humanly unimaginable perfection. Perfection indeed, more than mere spirituality, is the dominant predicate in the Islamic reference to God. Rather than associating the absence of divine speech with a space too large to be bridged between God and humans, Islam understands Allah's silence as belonging to a degree of divinity that does not allow for anthropomorphisms. A god speaking to human beings, we can extrapolate, would remind Muslims too much of their own life. If already Allah's distance appears incompatible with the precarious attempts of communication that we have identified as typical for the god of the Old Testament, to apply to the Islamic god a Christian idea of incarnation would likely be considered an act of blasphemy. For in the purest interpretation, the god of Islam has no organs, no voice, no words—strictly thinking, not even intentions or thoughts. Described from this perspective, Allah constitutes a void, a black hole of images—and also of concepts.

Consequently, the Quran as Islam's holy book cannot present itself as a history based on memories of God's interventions and words in the human world, as does the Old Testament and, under different premises and conditions, also the New Testament. Genealogically, in a sense slightly different from the Western intellectual concept, the Quran claims to go back to discourses about Allah that the archangel Gabriel, not God himself, conveyed to the Prophet Muhammad in a mountain cave between 610, when the prophet was forty years old, until his death in 632. Despite this view of its origin (that may well have shaped the range of its contents), the Muslims' holy book contains passages from the Torah and the gospel, referring to them as preliminary texts that go back to the "prophets": Moses, David, and Jesus. Presenting him as their final and definitive successor, the Quran describes Muhammad as *ummi*, that is "illiterate"—although the word's semantic complexity has led to different understandings. According to the Islamic tradition, Muhammad was preaching the knowledge he received from the archangel, while at the same time some of his followers had begun writing down what they had already heard from the prophet.

Some of those among Muhammad's followers, who had remembered by heart all of his words, died in a battle shortly after the prophet's death, so Abu Bakr, the first caliph, commissioned a written version of all available texts and fragments to assure their preservation. The widow of Muhammad was then entrusted with the manuscript, which explains why as early as around 650, the Quran's constitution as a written document reached its conclusion. Present-day Islamic scholarship indeed regards the Islam's holy book as identical with the manuscript compiled for Abu Bakr. Paradoxically, against the background of the prophet's supposed illiteracy and his intense preaching activity, the Quran as a written text has maintained a singular authority and stability throughout the centuries following its fast emergence. This status converges with the emphasis on Allah's perfection as the theological grounding of Islam. If God's omnipotence and perfection are taken literally, then both the text that his angel gave to the believers and the process of its compilation cannot allow for any doubts or variations. Any discussions about the historical process of transmission, let alone thoughts about an alternative process, would inevitably question Allah's perfection.

Inspired by these premises, there is a debate in Islamic theology about whether Muslims should believe in the Quran as "created" or as "uncreated." If imagining the Quran as created necessarily implies the idea of a time when Allah had not yet produced the words of the holy book, this opinion must take a step, too large a step for many believers, in associating him with human time. The other solution, the solution conceiving of the Quran as uncreated, makes the text part of God's eternal, that is non-temporal, existence. Quite plausibly, the second solution has come up with the idea of a "tablet" holding God's words in eternity, as opposed to a record of words spoken by his voice. Both views of the relation between God and the book are compatible with a self-image frequently coming up in the Quran of a book "sent to his Servant" (Surah 18: 1).[7] They both also endow the holy book with a closeness to God that requires rules for its treatment as a material object: readers shall wash their hands before they read a copy of the Quran, no other book can ever be put on top of the Quran, and Muslims do not regard translations to be identical with the Quran's Arabic text of origin.

Under the all-important premise of Allah's perfection and remoteness, the predominant speech situation that the text internally displays cannot be that of a god using his voice, and it thus features a discourse directed by a believer full of wisdom and experience "in the Name of Allah, the Most Compassionate, Most Merciful" to fellow believers who trusts his guidance: "This Book, without any doubt, is a guidance for those who fear God" (Surah 2: 1). Within its larger framework, the Quran displays different situations between speakers and listeners, and they are connected to multiple genres and types of content. All these elements, however, never come together in the linearity of one narrative or of one argument. More than any other textual dimension, it probably is the form of its rhythmic and frequently rhyming prose that gives the book an impressive coherence.

Invoking the Quran as "the Book that He has sent down upon you in truth," the third Surah recommends the readers refrain from interpreting it, admitting that many of the verses are "dark." Those who do seek their interpretation seek "discord" because "no one knows its meaning except Allah" (Surah 3: 5). While some other passages refer to the "verses basic and fundamental" as "explained in detail by one who is Wise and Well-Acquainted" (Surah 11:1), the resolute advice against interpretation has become dominant in the religious practice among Muslims. Rather than activating further thoughts or even debates, to follow God's words means to repeat them in reading, reciting, and listening. And repetition thus emerged as the prevalent Islamic modality of prayer that does not happen as a conversation with God but as an execution of the text that God has given to his faithful.

The consequences of that idea—that for God to speak to humans would be a degrading anthropomorphism—can hardly be overstated in their impact on the theology and religious practices of Islam. From a cultural theory perspective, they prove that the otherwise widespread association of divine figures with notions of a voice by no means deserves the status of a psychic, let alone a logical, necessity.

On the contrary—and without questioning the impact of teaching and rituals for Muslims—the absence of God's voice may well have been responsible for the particularly firm attitudes and practices that characterize Islam.

In Judaism and Christianity, the desire to endow transcendent authorities with a voice has survived the age of secularization—and even found a new existential place. For while it seems difficult to imagine human existence without the effects and the function in our psyche of what we call the "voice of conscience," this instance has acquired a historically new prominence due to secularization as a historical process following the Enlightenment. When we speak of "conscience," we invariably refer to an impulse that, on the one hand, mostly evades and even goes against our individual volition, agency, or plans, often with an effect of urgency, while, on the other hand, it has a power of command that we cannot possibly ignore—and to whose voice we can*not* not listen. Agreement or convergence between the directions of individual agency and of conscience—what we call "a good conscience"—seems to be the exception and quite regularly falls under the suspicion of self-complacency.[8] Typically conscience is an impulse that transcends and resists what we spontaneously, or after a process of reflection, want to do; and cultures have long associated conscience with different forms of divine intervention. But ever since a belief in God has ceased to be a general premise of existence, conscience has become for many of us a quite literally "transcendent" and at the same time secular component of existence.

In the twenty-fifth of his lectures held between 1915 and 1917 under the title "Introduction to Psychoanalysis," Sigmund Freud came up with a strictly secular description of conscience (*Gewissen*) as part of the superego's function of self-observation, more precisely as self-observation with the effect of censorship, originating in the "influence of parents, educators and social environment." The young Freud would probably have been delighted to know that today's experimental neuroscience has given an anatomical and physiological reality to conscience by locating its impulses in the anterior prefrontal cortex and by showing that accidents or surgical interventions can result in a loss or a weakening of the behavioral inhibitions that psychoanalysis refers to as the "censorship" of conscience.

We find an epistemologically quite different reality claim for conscience at the beginning of the chapter "Dasein's Attestation of an Authentic Potentiality-for-Being" in Martin Heidegger's *Being and Time*. In this work, Heidegger excludes conscience from the "present-at-hand" world outside the human mind, and instead identifies the "voice of conscience" as a "primordial phenomenon of existence" (*"ein ursprüngliches Phänomen des Daseins"*).

Although the expression "voice of conscience" seems to be present in most, if not all, Western languages, different individuals "hear" and describe its articulation in distinctively different ways. For my colleague Greicy from Curitiba in Brazil, she hears conscience as a clearly masculine voice, whereas Eva, a student at the Hebrew University, says that she always perceives conscience "as a whisper." But like all other voices of transcendence, the voices of conscience are not individualized, meaning they do not exhibit a "grain." This association with acoustic neutrality once again leads to the question of why we tend to connect instances of transcendent authority, in this case conscience, with the imagination of a speaking voice—more than with any other organ of the human body or with any other sensory modality. And why do we not instead attribute vocal effects to moments of thinking, of joy, or of pain?

Freud, who in general does not show much interest in the convergence between conscience and voice, exclusively mentions this connection as a function of the superego under the condition of "diseases of paranoia," which means as a pathological form of acoustic hallucination. In his essay "Introducing Narcissism" from 1914, he describes how paranoid "patients complain that all of their thoughts are known, all of their actions observed and monitored; voices inform them about the process of this authority" (*"sie werden von dem Walten dieser Instanz durch Stimmen informiert"*).[9]

Heidegger, by contrast, pays attention to the voice effect as shared by humans in general when he analyzes conscience as "a primordial phenomenon of existence." According to him, conscience and its voice always function as a possibility of bringing us back from a state of alienation, from the "everyday average fallenness to the They" ("Verfallenheit an das Man") to "one's own Self" ("zurück zum eigenen Selbst")—that is, back to a potential state of agency.

Heidegger refers to this function of bringing back humans from fallenness with the word "call" (*Ruf*) that is semantically inseparable from "voice" and adds a distinction between two German verbs that use *Ruf* as their basis. Conscience "summons" existence (*auf-rufen*), but conscience also "addresses" existence (*zu-rufen*). When considering the reason for the association between voice and conscience, the second meaning (*zu-rufen*) turns out to be more relevant because it attributes a personal directedness and an urgency to the call, whereas *auf-rufen* ("to summon") just announces, on a general level, that existential tasks will be at stake in the future. The personal directedness of *zu-rufen*, which Heidegger does not want to be misunderstood as "just . . . a 'picture,'" goes along with "the momentum of a push—of an abrupt arousal," and ultimately with forceful changes in our attitudes and our moods.[10] If, however, voice, call, *zu-rufen*, as directed to individual existence, play an important existential role by causing sudden discontinuities in our moods and in our relation to our own Self, then we can indeed assume, as *Being and Time* suggests, that specific articulated content loses pertinence in the voice of conscience. Heidegger goes so far—too far perhaps—as to write that "taken strictly" the call of conscience "has nothing to tell" and that therefore "conscience discourses solely and constantly in the mode of keeping silent." The expressionist style of 1920s Germany permeates these reflections and may have gone too far in its interpretation of the call of conscience when it deemphasized content by using the blatant paradox of a conscience that "discourses in the mode of keeping silent" ("das Gewissen redet einzig und ständig im Modus des Schweigens"). And yet Heidegger's description aligns with our impression that voices of religious transcendence tend to pay less attention to the content dimension.

We thus begin to understand how personal directedness, how what we can call "address," functions as a main component of what so many of us expect from divine voices and from the voice of conscience. Heidegger uses a particularly dramatic metaphor for this effect of personal appeal, address, and directedness: "While the content of the call is seemingly indefinite, the direction it takes is a sure one and is not to be overlooked." The German word behind "direction" in the English version of *Being and Time*[11] is the much stronger compound noun *Einschlagsrichtung*, aa a ballistic and often military metaphor that brings together direction with a physical impact or indeed with a hit, and thus makes readers think of a bullet. Compared to such power in the directedness of the call of conscience—the result of "hearing" and of interpreting the call—whether or not there can be hearing without content is supposed to remain vague and inconclusive. Above all, *Einschlagsrichtung* gives to the voice of conscience a connotation of reality outside the dimension of acoustics. And such a non-acoustic reality association may be one reason why we tend to connect voices with transcendental power although we cannot attribute any acoustic specificity to them.

There is no point in exploring the biographical or even political background that may have motivated Heidegger to choose a word like *Einschlagsrichtung* to illustrate what he found decisive about the voice of conscience, all the more so as such investigations often lead to unpleasant or off-putting results in his case. And yet, taking into account the analysis of conscience as "a primordial phenomenon of existence" in *Being and Time* enables us to grasp and define a new motif that is essential for our process of unfolding aspects and functions of the human voice in general, a motif that has disclosed itself along our way of reviewing voices of transcendent authority.

Without being aware of it and regardless of content, humans seem to enjoy and even desire the feeling of being personally addressed by voices; this may be another explanation for the obsession of attributing voices to gods and to the impulses of conscience. Now "address" is a function not exclusively covered by voices (we can "address" another person with a smile), but it is difficult to imagine a voice without the effect of address. We wish for voices to call and address us as individuals, the more intensely the better. If conscience as a function in our psyche did not produce the impression of a voice calling with its *Einschlagsrichtung*, it would probably be less successful in engaging us individually and in prompting us to behave differently. Due to the effect of personal address associated with divine voices, religious texts often have them invoke the names of those humans to whom they will be speaking: "Moses, Moses!" are the first two words that God speaks in Exodus, still out of the burning bush. And we are longing for such personal address even if we anticipate that it may also trigger feelings of embarrassment, fear, and guilt.

But how exactly do voices manage to give us a sense, if not a certainty, of being personally addressed? There is reason to doubt that this effect and our reactions to it have much to do with articulated content or with individual sound profiles. Could the effect and the reaction to it perhaps belong to an elementary level of sociability where voices surrounding us still maintain a neutrality, similar to the neutrality that we associate with the voices of gods and with the voice of conscience? Before we concentrate on meanings or on particular profiles of sounds, we attribute intentions—that is, the dynamic of a will to human voices—and refer such imagined intentions of others to ourselves. Without this projection of a will, we could not feel addressed and called by voices speaking in languages that we don't know or whose expressions we have not yet begun to understand. Such structures of personal address and directedness require the physical substance of real sound to function. Only real sound interrupts our focus on other objects of perception; only through real sound does an address become a movement in space that reaches and affects our bodies. Due to the sheer presence of physical voices in our environment, we may feel called—and are potential social beings even before we start to interact.

This could also be the reason for the human longing for a personal address from the gods that we imagine and the reason that makes us attribute voices with neutral perfection to them, independently of their revelations and commandments—even though we now understand that concepts of God have no absolute need for a voice. Unavoidably, however, this impulse also produces frustration and agony because, to truly satisfy our longing for personal address, the neutral voices of transcendence would need a physical substance that they cannot offer. Should we then say, half ironically, that it is a bad idea to make the address of transcendent authorities depend on voices? One response to the dilemma, the secular response, lies in the attention and authority that most of us give to the voice of conscience as an inner, secular, and different transcendental voice. Religious cultures provide the other, far more expansive response to our desire for transcendental address, and they do so without having to establish that divine voices are physically real voices. We could probably say that some religions, in their entirety, function as complex compensations for the energy of personal address that their gods cannot provide.

With the focus on voices of transcendental authority, it has become apparent how two profoundly different attempts to cope with their absence as a physical reality have shaped the theology and the religious practice of both Judaism and Christianity. Beside the fleeting presence of the word *kol* and of the "voice-thing" as its potential referent, the Torah's parallel existence as God's word in a written text and as God's word in the voice-involving human process of reading and interpretation has emerged as the Jewish way of coming to terms with the challenge. Incarnation in the figure of Jesus Christ, the paradox of trinitarian monotheism, and priesthood as delegation of the divine privilege of incarnation to human voices make up the Christian alternative.

Our attempt to deal with different ways of connecting voices to figures and functions of transcendental authority has produced some surprising perspectives on the Judeo-Christian legacy. The question of why so many religions let the authority of gods depend on voices, together with the insight that endowing gods with voices is by no means an inevitable function for human societies, brought us to the voiceless god of Islam. Without a divine voice, Islam strongly competes with Judaism and with Christianity in terms of global resonance and in the strong impression of personal address that it provides to its faithful.

———— SEVEN

Overwhelming Voices

AN UNCONCEALMENT OF CLOSENESS

AT THE BEGINNING OF THIS BOOK, I evoked my father's way of speaking as the main reason for a lasting fascination with human voices. That memory has held together the different aspects of these reflections in their surprising divergence, along with my father's feminine-sounding voice and the blurry imaginings with which I reacted to it being a source of pain during childhood and adolescence. The final chapter tries to provide an intellectual counterpoint in the existentially opposite tonality. It focuses on five voices from popular music that have given me a sense of closeness and of being able to hold onto them, a sense that I find largely physical and strangely reliable, despite its vagueness. At the same time, it is quite difficult to say where this impression of closeness comes from and what it can do, not only for me. To mention that certain singing voices have helped me through situations of precarity seems narratively adequate but does not explain the intuition that they belong to a primordial part of my existence, apart from active thinking or agency. Nor do such stories about problems overcome include my sense of being *overwhelmed*—that is, overwhelmed with pleasure—by those voices. Paradoxically somehow, I cannot imagine the past, the present, and the remaining future of my life without them, while I am incapable of describing what I would have missed in their absence. This exactly is the question that I pursue in concluding my thoughts about the lives of the voice.

The names related to the five overwhelming voices I will deal with are—in the biographical order of encountering them and, strangely somehow, without any ambiguities or doubts—Elvis Presley, Edith Piaf, Janis Joplin, Whitney Houston, and Adele. They all were—and are—part of what we call, condescendingly or not, popular culture and thus simply reflect, on the one hand, my own lack of familiarity with more elevated and culturally canonized echelons of music. On the other hand, their genre status implies an affinity to some general features of the human voice that determine its place within our existence. From a performance perspective, voices in popular music are not expected to excel thanks to any specific training, as opera voices do, and thus strike us as exhibiting what most voices can achieve, while, from the angle of reception and since the invention of sound recording, they have reached far greater numbers of listeners than spoken voices ever did.

Estimates for individual acts of listening to the most popular singing voices go into the hundreds of millions and even billions, which indeed makes them the quantitatively dominant reality of voice behavior in present-day culture, a rank elevated by the condition that recorded voices quite literally survive the bodies of which they were a part. Almost half a century after his death, Elvis Presley's is still among the most frequently heard voices worldwide. Under these premises, premises that are, as so often with voice phenomena, unsurprising but hardly ever mentioned, I assume that my own reactions to great voices belong to a broader range of the social average and that self-observation may again be a possible way to extrapolate some insights of more than just individual validity. In other words, I trust that my association of such popular voices with an elementary sense of closeness and hold is shared broadly enough to serve as an opening for some reflections about a both underlying and overarching dimension in our behavior, a dimension that is perhaps metahistorical and transcultural, always welcome, often desired, and seldom acknowledged.

The attempt to find out what I would have missed in my life without those favorite voices proceeds in three parts. I start by bringing together concepts and theory elements developed throughout the previous chapters into a larger description of listening to popular songs, a description geared to understand what we mean when we are saying that we like to "hold onto" them. On this basis and in the middle of the chapter, I narrate—through a series of case studies illustrating what "lives of voices" can be—how my histories with the voices of Elvis Presley, Edith Piaf, Janis Joplin, Whitney Houston, and Adele, with their individually different modes of acoustic sensuality, have converged in yielding an elementary sense of substance and union for me that is difficult to describe in experiential terms.

Rather than as a specific kind of experience, I propose interpreting the impact of such voices as the *unconcealment of a general closeness* to other humans in their primary physical being, a closeness not regulated by instinct in the sense of what happens with animals, a closeness that we cannot help participating in although we hardly ever notice it. Being a basic condition that we cannot bypass or leave behind, that primary closeness never truly becomes an object of our experience as something that we see "from outside." Applied to moments in life where we don't have such an objective perspective and where phenomena are supposed "to show themselves" instead of being discovered, Martin Heidegger's concept of "unconcealment" can help us grasp what voices invariably are for us and why it is worthwhile to go as far as possible in describing them.

Although I am approaching this most ambitious level in my analysis of voices by focusing on popular songs, I am not insisting that this is the preferred or the only perspective to apply. Popular songs have simply been my own most frequent and most impactful way of participating in the lives of the voice.

Singing voices affect us with the three ontologically diverse and yet functionally intertwined effects we have referred to as "the knot of voice": with sequences of sound waves touching our bodies, with propositional content that the sound waves articulate, and with fluid movements of the imaginary triggered by both sounds and meanings. But singing voices also affect us with the music inherent in their articulation and sometimes emphasized by instruments that accompany the vocal performance. We can say that, in the case of singing, the knot of the voice and music are the two components of a synesthetic relationship that produces complex effects. For the performing voice itself, melodies as combinations of rhythms and pitch normally bring to our acoustic attention a broader variety of high and low tones than spoken language, which intensifies their appeal. More often than in opera voices, however, whose main cultural function lies in extending the customary range of tonal performance, voices in popular songs occasionally suspend their synchronization with music and then produce what we call the melodramatic effect of words spoken against instrumental music as their background.

To those who sing and to those who hear singing voices, the music carrying them, through the different media technologies, activates an emotional disposition of increased excitability bordering on euphoria, of openness toward the surrounding world and to internal impulses of pleasure, a disposition capable also of soothing and even of easing feelings of pain. Offering a broader spectrum of sounds than speaking voices, singing voices also provoke a particular intensity of psychic resonance. At the same time, due to melody, they are connected to and shaped by rhythms that resonate with the temporality of the listeners' reactions to them: the rhythm of the listening gets progressively adapted to the rhythm of the voice heard. If, as we have said, rhythms are practical solutions to the problem of how time objects in the proper sense (voice articulations, for example) can have a stable form, then they attenuate the impression of their unfolding as sequences of subsequent sounds. We indeed tend to remember voices as if they were atemporal phenomena, and this difference between their actual articulation and their form in our remembering may be one reason for their infamous lack of precision, even among specialists, in the discourses characterizing individual voices.

A second effect that we have associated with voice articulations in rhythmic structure is the impression that they conjure up the situations, objects, or persons they refer to with a concreteness that seems to make them palpable. Could such concreteness be a reason behind the impression of singing voices as something to "hold onto"—although they obviously are not the material objects that a listener can grasp? Such imagined external concreteness may converge with the psychologically internal concreteness called mood (*Stimmung*) that moments of light physical touch on our bodies, such as a singing voice, can provoke. Tony Morrison once characterized mood as a sense "like being touched from inside," giving it a strong physical connotation. Together, the broader range of tones that singing voices have in comparison to spoken language, the heightened degree of resonance they evoke, and the two converging impulses of concreteness triggered by them in our imagination account for a sometimes-profound impact.

But we also need to remember that singing in general reverses the standard relation between the sound of voices and the propositional content whose presence we take for granted in our everyday conversations and in the existential spaces emerging from them. Instead of primarily articulating meaning, as spoken texts normally do, songs turn the meaning of their lyrics into forms that facilitate the showcasing of voices—otherwise we would never listen to songs performed in languages we don't understand. Due to this different status of language as "tonal grounding" and no longer as content-producing "gestural symbolic," to quote Friedrich Nietzsche,[1] meanings tend to lose their contours in songs. Pleasure and pain, we have seen, no longer stand in contrast on this level, which is why popular songs show a preference for bittersweet motifs. Distinctions in general, including gender distinctions, lose the clarity we rely on in most everyday situations—which is probably why I cannot say that feminine voices impress me in ways fundamentally different from the impact of masculine voices. The double-sided concreteness activated by songs in the listeners' minds thus becomes a concreteness without form, an unspecific palpability. We sense that we can hold onto something without knowing what this something may be in each individual case.

Like any other acoustic impulse, the perception of songs activates both the visual and the tactile modality of our imagination. But compared to spoken voices, the visual and tactile imagery triggered by singing voices appears less certain. Even if, in a live performance or in a recording, we do see the body to which a voice belongs and therefore no longer depend on visual imagination, the tactile imagination triggered by songs maintains an ambiguity. While songs may make us sensitive to such impulses of tactile imagination, they normally don't give us the impression of being touched by somebody specific. Being thus an effect of vague contours, the impression of palpability conjured up by songs does not conflict with possible forms of self-reference. Rather, our imaginary and its physical connotations merge with the open palpability evoked by voices and become part of it. The sense of holding onto voices may well belong to an all-embracing state of bodily concreteness into which we like to immerse ourselves.

So far, I have exclusively focused on reactions, emotions, and impulses that recorded voices of popular music can trigger in individuals listening to them. What further insights and concepts will a broader social focus on that type of situation yield? To make this question viable, we need to revise the conventional meaning of the word "social." Listening to recorded voices will never produce what we have called "existential spaces" because the persons who own these voices do not react to those who enjoy hearing them. Nor will recorded voices typically trigger strong impulses to sing along, as live voices do, because we aren't in a "lateral" position with the singers' bodies, a position necessary for the activation of mirror neurons and their copying effects. Instead of really singing along, we often "hum along" with recordings or we vocalize fragments of their lyrics, but such moments cannot lead to the emergence of "mystical bodies"—that is, to the specific form of sociability that includes human bodies. Paradoxically, listening to recorded voices is a social situation that happens in solitude.

However, what this situation of solitude shares with that of existential spaces is an asymmetry between the high level of attention dedicated to the objects of outside perception and the formlessness of self-observation. As for our attention to outside perception (everything we notice that is not self-observation), with today's technology voice recordings are indeed capable of producing a physical impact equivalent to the impact of voices that we hear in our actual presence and that thus influence our bodies and minds. In addition, and despite the solitude of listening to recordings, we also associate a lighter mode of address with singing voices in general—that is, the counterintuitive impression that they are personally directed to us. By contrast, in terms of self-observation, our focus remains unspecific while we listen to recorded voices, unspecific to a degree that is no longer compatible with a state of subjecthood and agency. This may be yet another reason for the impression that we merge with our favorite voices.

Consequently, the strong emotional reactions that recorded voices often provoke are hardly ever processed by a coherent form of self-awareness or agency. Instead, our minds react with states of multilayered expansion. We imagine the bodies of vocal artists and their movements, we project desires and memories onto these imagined bodies, and we often associate with their songs what we believe to know about the historical worlds to which they pertain. As we never get any resistance to such strong associations, recorded songs can conjure up certain times in our lives with their specific horizons of knowledge, emotions, and wishes. If the desire to listen to new songs has at first some level of addiction, we later develop the enjoyable habit of returning with them to different stages and moments of our individual past. This a type of lived experience embodied—in my case, by the voices of Elvis Presley, Edith Piaf, Janis Joplin, Whitney Houston, and Adele—that does not necessarily have the structure of personal histories, although it is possible to narrate our lives along their sequence. Full of wide-ranging, uncontrolled projections and memories that they absorb and preserve, recorded voices can become a presence that gives a sense of substance and undefined union to our own existence.

While five famous voices from an extended period of popular music are of exceptional importance to me, I have never closely followed the surrounding production and performance industry and thus did not necessarily connect with them when these artists' voices were in everybody's ears. My encounters with these voices have more to do with the changing desires and challenges of my life—as well as some obvious randomness. There are probably no inevitable patterns, let alone possible theories, for how we handle such voices. What matters—and what I hope I will be able to evoke—is their soft energy, their palpability, and their open-endedness as a horizon and a substance of existence.

When, twenty-three years old and already peaking in his worldwide popularity, Elvis Presley arrived at the German harbor city of Bremerhaven on October 1, 1958, to pass eighteen months of military service in the American Army, I had just started my gymnasium education. Latin was my first foreign language, and I felt that I needed to devote many hours a day of hard studying and concentration due to my lack of natural ability. Like many classmates, I had received a transistor radio as a present from my parents and loved getting into bed at night and secretly listening to programs of popular music, mainly to American Forces Network (AFN), then the most accessible radio station in southern Germany. Although I did not understand a word of English, I was as fascinated by the announcer's deep, and for me, exotically melodious voice as I was by Paul Anka's "Diana," my earliest favorite song.

This pleasure reached a different level of intensity with Elvis Presley's presence on the old continent. I had occasionally heard his name mentioned on AFN and liked some of his hits with their still unfamiliar rock 'n' roll beat, above all "Jailhouse Rock" and "King Creole"—this was partly in silent protest, because my mother talked about these songs as proof of a lack of taste, if not decadence, in American culture. Elvis Presley gave AFN a new tone of pride and prestige, with each song occupying center stage on the different daily shows. One late evening in my bed, I heard "Don't" for the first time, whose slow melody and richness would attach me to Elvis's voice for life. The word "don't," repeated four times at the beginning and also concluding the song, let this voice emerge with a dark beauty that captured my attention, gave me gooseflesh, and made me feel both pleasantly overwhelmed and happily sad when, after about three minutes, it vanished. Nothing seemed to be between Elvis's "Don't" and me; the song sounded natural and honest, with an unknown warmth of summer. During some brief moments in the middle of "Don't," the words turned to a solemnity of spoken language that, as an altar boy, reminded me of the Sunday morning High Mass, although they lacked the imposing seriousness I was used to from my religious world.

With "Don't," even my mother conceded that "Elvis Presley could sing." I dreamed that I could become this voice, although my voice had not become masculine yet. According to a story that I later heard my parents tell with surprising pride, I must have managed to learn by heart the lyrics of "Don't" (which I did not understand), to retain the melody, and to somehow perform the song to the encouraging and amused reactions of guests whom we had over for dinner. But at some point this practice must have become frustrating and embarrassing for me, because I obviously had no way to copy Elvis's voice, let alone to become "one" with it. What somehow emerged from this singularly captivating experience was a neverending appreciation and even an affection for Elvis. For all my self-imposed dedication to more canonized levels of culture, I followed with affective proximity the dramatic successes and failures of his life, quite passionately rooting for him to both remain "the King" and to have a happy family life. His struggles with prescription pills, body weight, and corrupt financial managers hurt me to the same extent as his triumphant return to stage performance in Las Vegas in 1969 became a reason for joy and admiration. The genre of songs for which I have an addiction never changes. Beside "Don't," the early "Love Me Tender," and "Can't Help Falling in Love" from 1961, "As Time Goes By" in the recording of Elvis's final stage appearance at the Market Square Arena in Indianapolis still deeply moves me. Each of these songs gives an overwhelmingly full presence to the aura, the range, and the volume of his voice.

During a stay in Rio de Janeiro, I heard about Elvis Presley's neither particularly surprising nor anticipated death on August 16, 1977, during a time when I found affection for American popular culture and for its visibly aging king incompatible with my political and intellectual ambitions. But while I did not want to betray a visible reaction to that piece of news, I Immediately knew how significant it was for me and how it provoked, for the first time, that somehow disproportionate question of how I could live without the beloved voice. No other death—neither other celebrities nor those of beloved relatives—had such a depressing impact on me. For several days, it was difficult to concentrate on work, on conversations with friends, or on the exuberantly beautiful landscape of Rio. Had I lost an anchor of existential security?

The following days confirmed existentially what I could have anticipated for practical reasons. Elvis's voice, which I had never heard live, remained present for me in its multiple recordings and on different radio stations. Life in the absence of Elvis Presley was possible, although something essential that I could not point to was gone. While I continued to listen to my favorite Elvis songs, his biography and its historical environments became objects of interest and soon also of study and writing for me, partly letting me understand why this voice had become so indispensable. It had accompanied my steps from childhood to being a person of my own, no longer controlled by parents. But there was also something uniquely American in those songs, a remote and yet familiar world that was still upbeat, at peace with and even fond of itself. Their tone also suggested the presence of African American culture—it wasn't by chance that the record industry had discovered Elvis Presley's voice as a "Black voice"— during a time when African Americans were still excluded from the mainstream audience that he, as a white man from the South, was able to conquer. After the peak of the Vietnam War around 1970, that treacherously beautiful world of social segregation and popular self-happiness became permeated by habitual self-doubt and permanent self-critique. In the final stage of his career, Elvis's voice conjured up an America that no longer existed.

I had refrained from admitting how fond I was of that voice and did not even admit to myself how much I longed for its softly overwhelming fullness and warmth. And yet its tone and all the connotations connected to it must have stayed strong in its bodily resonance because without it, I believe I would not have chosen, in the late 1980s, the United States as a new country for my family and myself—the place for my children and later my grandchildren to reside. Elvis's voice kept close that unnamed, much happier, and no-longer existing America.

When, a half decade after our permanent arrival in California, my wife and I decided to do the classic cross-country road trip with our four children, each of us was allowed to choose one place to add to the itinerary. My choice, without hesitation, was Graceland, Tennessee, the estate around the house that Elvis bought for his parents in 1957, where he died twenty years later, and where he is buried next to his mother. That day in that touristy environment and surrounded by Elvis's voice flowing through every room, I was again surprised—and still embarrassed—by the impact that it had on me after so many years. I was sobbing when I heard my favorite songs, overwhelmed by the intense power the songs had on me at Graceland, with reminders of Elvis's presence everywhere.

Probably due to how early it came into my life, the voice of Elvis Presley has been omnipresent and strangely difficult to grasp. The voice of Edith Piaf, by contrast, occupied and still holds a more specific, almost well-defined status in my life. Becoming aware, more through history classes at the gymnasium than from my family, of Germany's National Socialist past, which had ended three years before my birth, I felt the desire to embrace a different national legacy. With American culture having been so all-pervasive during my childhood years with the post-war occupation and therefore somehow undefined for me, at age fifteen I decided to learn French as a third foreign language to give me entry to a different, well-contoured otherness. Each French word that I learned to pronounce, each name of a French town or of a protagonist from French history, promised distance from the inherited Germanness. This obsession provoked disapproval among friends and teachers, which only strengthened my resolve to opt to spend the larger part of my final year before university with an Alsatian family in Paris; there, along with the family's five children, I attended a prestigious lycée and was enthusiastic about its intellectual climate and unaware of its institutional rank. Every day and every detail added to my longing for otherness.

Unlike what happened for me with Elvis Presley, I have no recollection of the moment when I first heard an Edith Piaf song. In my attempt to construct a French identity, which could never really become my own, I sought points of reference, and Edith Piaf's voice illustrated French existentialism—a philosophy, style, and everyday world that I associated with the French resistance against German occupation between 1940 and 1943. Her voice itself was also history, because she had died in 1963, forty-eight years old—long before I noticed and remembered her name. Edith Piaf thus first stood for a range of knowledge. Only later, when I finally listened to "La Vie en Rose," her signature song from 1945 that my hosts and teachers frequently mentioned, the physical immediacy of wanting to become one with her voice and its world took over, together with the happiness of leaving behind my original cultural background. In a different way than my earlier encounters with American popular music, I was able and eager to understand her lyrics, which gave a form to my immersion into Piaf's voice.

Above all, the first sentence in the refrain of "La Vie en Rose" determined how this voice touched me: "Quand il me prend dans ses bras / Qu'il me parle tout bas / Je vois la vie en rose." I knew that existentialist philosophy insisted on isolating the intense happiness of brief moments from their possibly negative and even devastating long-term consequences, that it emphasized and celebrated a transitory sense of fulfillment as the true meaning of life. The specific blissful tone of Piaf's songs, evoked against a shallow everydayness, gave her voice its fragile strength. And this motif became only more prominent and tender with a line, towards the end of the song and performed with particular emphasis, in which she reminds her lover how he had "sworn that love would last for life" ("Tu me l'as dit, m'as juré pour la vie"). I understood this reminder as yet another trace of endless insecurity and wanted to embrace and embody such triumphant precariousness myself, as it felt so much more sophisticated than the values of my upbringing.

Holding onto Piaf's triumphant fragility also became an alternative to the calm plenitude that Elvis Presley's songs had given me. She sounded like strength in awareness of unavoidable loss—although such thoughts and concepts only seldom became distinct meanings in the sound complexity of her voice, filled with emotion. Rather, her voice brought together all layers of meaning into one complex and multilayered presence.

Learning about the eccentric circumstances of Edith Piaf's life endowed this voice with even more authenticity. Her parents had been street performers, and she had spent part of her childhood years living in a bordello. As a public emblem of existentialism and of *la Résistance*, she had also been suspected of collaborating with the German enemy. Quite regularly, Edith Piaf's love affairs had turned into disappointment and even humiliation. The one moving exception was her love for Marcel Cerdan, a French professional boxer, whom she met during a tour through the United States in 1947. Two years later, Cerdan took a flight to see her in New York and died in a plane crash.

This one irrecuperable loss intensified the impression of deep precariousness that I heard in Edith Piaf's voice. Listening to "La Vie en Rose" became an immersion into existentialism with an immediacy that powerfully transcended an understanding of philosophical concepts and content. At the same time, being overwhelmed by her voice and losing my own self in it also seemed to blur the shape of the historical world from which her songs had emerged, opening up a horizon of associations where Piaf's voice merges with other voices of my life in a complex layer of palpability. With their sensual convergence, those songs also bring together the worlds they have absorbed, transforming different existential layers into one concrete dimension of relating to the world. In this dimension, the existentialist precarity of happiness that Edith Piaf's voice still embodies approaches the plenitude, the directness, and the happy American past of Elvis Presley's voice. They have become one core in my existence and yet maintain a different tonalities; they both suspend the distance between different parts of my life and keep tangible their sensual diversity.

Dreaming, since my adolescent years in Paris and later in Salamanca and in Pavia, of becoming a Romanist (that is, according to the German academic tradition, a specialist but also an enthusiast of the literatures and cultures of Romance languages), I never imagined that in the second part of my life I would enthusiastically become American by choice. Although I was unaware of it when I emigrated to California in 1989, the voices broadcast by AFN and stored in my memory must have made me feel like I was returning to my true existential home. Elvis Presley's songs, which had crystalized as my German impression of America, somehow anticipated my new life.

I needed a different American voice to follow, a voice that would attract and lead me towards new places with an unfamiliar way of living, and I found it in Janis Joplin's rendition of "Me and Bobby McGee" from 1971, which I had long admired among many other popular songs from my future country. The song indeed turned into a vocal bridge between the two halves of my life and has ever since become a favorite piece of music. Transforming into a sequence of sounds a trajectory onto the map of the United States, "Me and Bobby McGee" also is my personal American anthem. Its lyrics begin in the Deep South of Baton Rouge, Louisiana, with Janis feeling "busted flat" and "feelin' near as faded" as her jeans, in a dark, calm, and casual voice. No opening could be less ceremonious or un-opera-like, with her voice appearing all of a sudden and somehow at random. It goes with the same volume and pitch "all the way in to New Orleans" while Janis sings along with Bobby, her hitchhiking buddy, "every song that driver knew." Still calm and moving, the words "Freedom's just another word for nothin' left to lose" come up, leading to "the Kentucky coal mine to the California sun," with a greater insistence on sound and melody. The voice sounds hoarse and more individual now, as Janis "shared the secrets" of her soul while Bobby "kept" her "from the cold."

"One day up near Salinas" in California, her quiet happiness of having nothing left to lose collapses. She lets Bobby "slip away," and we hear from the pain in her voice how she hopes he finds "that home" he is looking for. She would "trade" all her "tomorrows for one single yesterday" of "holdin' Bobby's body" next to hers. There is nothing left to lose but the memory that being together "was good enough" for her and Bobby McGee. Whenever I listen to these words in Janis Joplin's voice, I become part of a story that is far away from my biographical life—and yet it is close in my memory of moving to America as I become absorbed by its sounds. The voice moves on to a long ending, abandoning all words and becoming one and alone with the music, a long and open ending without regret, without meaning, without any direction beyond it.

No other voice ever carries me so gently into a story, not by lyrics but in the sequence of its tones and its rhythms that touch my body. Each time I hear "Me and Bobby McGee," I am in a state that redeems all thinking and all longing for a different life. I am close to her voice in the absence of my own words, shape, or otherness. And while it overwhelms and brings me to that neverland of redemption, it also is the recorded voice of somebody dead in an individual fate and a far-away world. Born in Texas and having gone through every possible conflict of middle-class life, Janis Joplin ended up embodying the bright Californian dream of boundless freedom, of a freedom whose jolts and intensities became sheer presence in her voice and thus had nothing left to lose. It was the freedom for every sensual pleasure to be imagined, a freedom of expanding all limits of body and mind.

In Janis Joplin's voice, I sense yet another specifically American tone of living, dreaming, and dying that lasted for a few years between the beautifully naïve complacency of a nation proud of its rise and unaware of its scars and its collective frustration over promises impossible to forget and to fulfill. Nobody cared less about reason or convention than she did; her life was a crescendo of her most beautiful song—going from places like Texas, Hollywood, and Woodstock to her wordless death from a drug overdose in the Los Angeles hotel room, where, surrounded by fame and success, nobody was waiting for her anymore. Her life, so boundless and destructive over twenty-seven years, so aggressive with herself and sometimes with others, ended on October 4, 1970, which may have been the only way back to the calm and tender early voice that is still with us. The recorded voice keeps alive a closeness and energy that only she could produce—and she was not able to maintain. If there was nothing left to lose, not even her own life, Janis Joplin's voice, separate from her body, preserves a past too extreme to survive. With this voice on my mind and in my ears, I reached the second half of my life, and I am holding onto it on days of confusion and boredom, like a harmlessly efficient drug keeping present a long-vanished world of light and psychedelics. Janis Joplin's voice sounds stronger and more utopian when we know that death was its ultimate price.

Quite far away from the wounds of such existential extremes, as they have long come to rest in recordings and historical archives, our Californian existence has far exceeded my family's and my own expectations. We found the serenity of a home, a rhythm of daily joys, and the warmth of surrounding affection. The older children embraced their everyday with new friends, games, and assignments, and their younger brother grew up in the transparent light of mildly oscillating seasons. Seventeen months into our life near the Pacific, we proudly announced the birth of Laura Teresa, the first American citizen in the family. Living not far away from Hollywood, we also discovered the pleasure of going to the movies as often as we could find reliable-enough babysitters, with a preference for comedy and other light genres rather than trying to acquire any level of sophistication.

One of the pictures considered a "must" for intentionally average viewers in the early 1990s was *The Bodyguard* featuring Kevin Costner and, for the first time in a leading role on the big screen, Whitney Houston, whose voice had by then already reached global renown, and not only among fans of popular music. The plot's flatness matched all expectations for films made with the simple purpose of box office sales thanks to the names and faces of famous actors. Academy Award–nominated film and music superstar hires good-looking bodyguard to protect herself against the threats of a stalker, they fall in love while solving the criminal case and decide to separate because they don't trust that their relationship can work in the long run. There were several aspects of the film, though, that I found exceptional. As a love story, *The Bodyguard* begins by invoking a physical threat and, at the same time, a physical strength competent to minimize it. The title hero's final departure on a private airplane is postponed for one last passionate kiss, after which Whitney Houston, without much of a narrative transition, sings "I Will Always Love You," the one reason why we still remember the film. And her physical beauty and voice captured me in an unusually quiet way.

An "average romantic thriller drama," as a critic wrote at the time, the movie was a typical bittersweet romance with a beautiful actress, culminating in some unforgettable minutes with one of the greatest singing voices ever. Unlike Janis Joplin's "Me and Bobby McGee," neither the lyrics nor the tonal structure of Whitney Houston's "I Will Always Love You" unfold narratively. They begin with words spoken in melodramatic seriousness, words that by mere association establish a link to the story told by the film: "If I should stay / I would only be in your way. / So I'll go, but I know / I'll think of you every step of the way." These two sentences do indeed express a bittersweet mood; the word "bittersweet" itself comes up in the next melodramatic passage: the mood that Nietzsche believed to belong to an archaic layer of the human psyche, a mood also blurring all meaning-producing distinctions. Thus each time I hear Whitney Houston's voice sing these words about a parting that defies her impulse to love, it impacts me physically, even though I never really process the words' ambiguous meaning. Her voice touches me as a caressing sound, lighter than the touch of a hand and yet with great emotional depth.

Without a transition or contrast, the voice then rises to a strength where the touch becomes an embrace that surrounds me, keeping its tenderness and warmth, giving me goose bumps, and losing all shapes of meaning in the repetition of the same sentence: "And I will always love you / I will always love you." As the forms of meaning vanish, Whitney Houston's voice alone fills my perception, extending the sounds of some vowels into oscillating melismas that never lose softness. If, like my other favorite voices, it overwhelms me with its warm power and invites me to lose myself in its embrace, it also continues to address me and thus keeps my presence alive. I feel its closeness because it never absorbs the space for my body, and I want to inhabit this space that is no longer a space of solitude. I want to stay there, "always." The floating contrast between melodramatic words spoken and Whitney Houston's singing in its full beautiful strength comes back two more times, making even greater the pleasure of being embraced without losing oneself.

The song closes with several musical variations and syntactical repetitions of the sentence "I will always love you." Love is not a theme anymore; the voice becomes love instead. It becomes as a bodily proximity giving me space. That this is an African American voice has always mattered to me, because I naïvely long to be part of the entire culture, country, nation, and society that I chose—in all of its exciting diversity. And yet the voice of Whitney Houston seems to have no individual or cultural limits; it feels like a caressing closeness from all others and for all others, which became a presence of love in the middle of my life that I have ever since desired to remain intense and fulfilling.

Among my dearest voices, Whitney Houston's is the one chronologically closest to me. Fifteen years older than her, I early on felt pride over the growing, soon worldwide success of her singing, and this acclaim first gave me a sense of how difficult it is to describe individual voices. Reading in the *New York Times* that Houston's voice was "a technical marvel from its velvety depths to its ballistic middle register to its ringing and airy heights"[2] and in *Rolling Stone* that it showcased "bone-deep feeling and technical perfection,"[3] I felt that these descriptions were simultaneously both adequate and not precise enough. However, the only discursive alternative I have ever seen is to try to capture the reactions that voices produce—instead of their physical and musical reality. From reading the biographical details of Whitney Houston, I learned that she had received a classical education, under the ambitious tutelage of her mother, and sang gospel music with her church, but this information doesn't bring me any closer to understanding my reactions. All I can say is that when I listen to this voice, remembering and imagining its performance have become existentially vital, perhaps even indispensable for me, without any definable reason.

Following her career with admiration and love also meant that news about her declining public resonance or about struggles in her private life deeply saddened me. But while I had the common reaction of shock and sympathy when I read that her marriage had deteriorated into abusiveness, I was also aware that this revelation intensified my appreciation for the sheer beautify of her voice. Not only did she turn a song like "I Will Always Love You" into a presence of love, but her voice resonated with her individual pain.

Whitney Houston's death on February 11, 2012, impressed me as much as Elvis Presley's death thirty-five years earlier, although it provoked quite different emotions. Although I now knew that, thanks to recordings, I would never lose her caressing voice, there was an impulse not to accept that she had drowned in a bathtub of the Beverly Hilton Hotel due to the effects of heart disease and cocaine use. This was not even a dramatic or exceptional, let alone heroic, by contemporary media coverage standards; it was a death not nearly worthy of so much beauty. The funeral service one week later in her home state of New Jersey brought together relatives, friends, colleagues, and, remotely, a nation of true admirers. Kevin Costner eulogized her with affection and sadness more poignantly than any script could have. After twenty years "I Will Always Love You" rose to number three on the Billboard charts again. More even than regret and sorrow, I felt consolation and gratitude remembering that such beauty had been possible at all. And it is still with us.

All these beloved voices came into my life at specific moments and for specific reasons, but they have stayed with me simultaneously, in their different moods with their bodily resonance, rather than in a chronological history of individual memories. They have become a substance of life without internal distinctions. While, for example, I recall the years when Whitney Houston's voice was so important to me as representative of a wide optimism that now looks like an illusion, its sound has turned into a promise of love's fulfillment merged with more somber tones of life's reality.

I first heard Adele's songs through my children, who are of her generation. I was then around sixty years old, finding myself without clear-cut professional plans and in a state of shameful weakness about my emotional attachments. I was feeling shallow, unable to embrace the potential of the beautiful existence that I had, and yet I was unwilling to consider that this was life's climax. There was no hint that I might expect help from the voice of a woman young enough to be my daughter and too far away in style and mood to catch my interest. Then, during three months of a fellowship stay in Berlin in 2012, my spiraling aimlessness turned into fear and depression. Mostly alone and thus confronted with myself, I realized that I had let disintegrate the loving close relationship that had been holding me throughout my life.

I had no idea how I could come back to that love. All I had left was the daily routine of continuing to exist, without any motivation or grounding, and not much more than being too cowardly to take my own life. Getting up felt like a challenge every morning, as I had no energy to leave the unconsciousness of sleep and to enter the world without any appeal for me. In that state I randomly heard "Someone Like You," the Adele song that, released in January 2011, had first brought her global acclaim and was then omnipresence in European and North American media. I had most probably listened to it before, but now I suddenly knew that this voice could help me make the transition from sleep and unconsciousness into each new day—and thus fulfill a much timelier function than any of my other favorite voices.

And this is exactly how I functioned for several more weeks, with no other changes in sight. Before any other activity, I would listen to "Someone Like You" after waking up every morning, and the almost five minutes of the recording always included the seconds of getting out of bed and onto my feet. If "Someone Like You" dwells on a specific mood instead of narrating a story, the first moments, like those of "Me and Bobby McGee," give the impression of joining conversation an ongoing conversation: "I heard that you're settled down / That you found a girl and you're married now / I heard that your dreams came true / Guess she gave you things, I didn't give to you." The situation conjured up by these words had little to do with my own. Rather than being abandoned and forgotten, my love had gone astray and into a state of dissolution due to a lack of care and affection for which I alone was responsible. Instead of a chance to identify, Adele's voice just offered me the continuity of its tone with little movement or variation: a tone from afar and of solitude, with no hope or promise, husky from lasting pain and acceptance of fate. That voice had neither hopeful illusions nor a threat of greater disappointment. It stubbornly remained aware of an ending that had irreversibly happened. And this stubbornness of Adele's voice carried me from waking up into the early day, every morning, during those weeks of emptiness when my bittersweet memories had turned pale. Instead of oscillating in an ambiguity of moods, which "Someone Like You" also explicitly mentions, the voice presided over a paradoxical union of fading and lasting.

As I am writing these lines, Adele is thirty-five years old; her voice is everywhere and promises to last far into the future. She now seems to have a happy private life, mostly secluded from media attention and from the curiosity of her fans. Is her voice the one exception, signaling a troubled existence as a gesture of authenticity? Perhaps Adele and her production team handle the relationship between voice and private life with a new level of insight and reflection, for example, by emphasizing an overlap between the songs and her real existence.

Adele's early and most successful albums are titled with numbers that refer to the age she was when she wrote their songs. The album *21*, for instance, contains "Someone Like You," which Adele describes as being inspired by a major breakup in her life. This disclosure went along with allusions to earlier difficult times she had been through, like growing up without a father or having problems with alcohol during her adolescent years. But we also get the impression of a well-thought-out strategy in the episodes and images from her life that she allows to circulate. Should we assume that an appearance of being grounded in personal pain, wounds, and scars has promoted the success of her songs? Would the brand of Adele's voice suffer if her life turned into a publicly displayed—and publicly confessed—state of unambiguous happiness?

I will never forget how this voice helped me to continue my life in the middle of confusion and despair a decade ago. Meanwhile, for me, "Someone Like You" represents an abstract potential of will and stubborn energy against all odds. And while this energy does not represent an existential endpoint, I have stopped finding new favorite voices.

For the longest time, it was impossible to imagine my life without the voices of Elvis Presley, Edith Piaf, Janis Joplin, Whitney Houston, and Adele, although I could not say why listening to them mattered so much. The attempt to find out, for each case, how and why these voices were indispensable has revealed some recurring conditions for their functions and for their emergence. They all became important in moments of personal transition or instability by giving me the vague and yet emotionally reassuring impression of being able to hold onto them, and they all ended up existing independently of the moments and circumstances of their first impact, merging into a layer of feelings and moods that I experience as substantial for my existence. With Elvis Presley's voice on the transistor radio, I went from childhood to early adolescence; Edith Piaf's songs accompanied my entry into adulthood outside my culture of origin; "Me and Bobby McGee" in Janis Joplin's voice became a trajectory towards my new American life; Whitney Houston's voice helped me find love and plenitude during my early years in the United States; and listening to Adele's "Someone Like You" kept me alive during a period of loss and depression.

While I have no conception of a common denominator for all these situations and while their challenges and dramas were quite different, a curious sense of spiritual closeness was significant in each of them. This is why I said that my favorite voices overwhelmed me in a soft and mostly pleasant manner. But what precisely can that mean? Being overwhelmed is certainly not a form of social interaction where people exchange knowledge, coordinate their ways of behaving, or compete among themselves. When we speak of being overwhelmed, we mean that our personality temporarily loses its shape while being absorbed by a different personality whose contours remain in place and substitute for ours. We can react with positive or with negative emotions to this process, we can affirm and desire it or try to resist and interrupt it. Being overwhelmed and absorbed by beautiful voices obviously belongs to those existential situations that we often search for and experience with pleasure. At the same time, they always affect, to some degree, both the mental and the bodily dimensions of our lives. When we feel absorbed by another person's voice, we inevitably have the impression of physically merging, of becoming part of, with our entire bodies, movements and vibrations belonging to another person's body.

Of course, we have to consider the dimension of gender difference when we talk about a merging between bodies. Its pertinence becomes particularly evident as soon as we acknowledge that today's attempts at conceptual and phenomenological distinctions challenge both the inertia of the predominant everyday belief that we can easily tell apart feminine from masculine voices and also the more apparently objective anatomical divergences between them. We should therefore connect the insights from previous chapters about existential effects unfolding from the knot of the voice with the question of whether those insights have identified any functions exclusively related to different voice types based on binary or more complex gender distinctions.

Regarding the five singing voices I have described that have had an overwhelming impact on myself—a man with an old-fashioned "straight" self-image—the predominance of women's voices seems to lead to the conclusion that an erotic component plays a decisive role. After all, Elvis Presley, the one male exception among my favorite vocalists, goes back to a pre-adolescent stage in my life. But while I am not aware of having any interest in denying such an erotic attraction coming from the voices of women, I have already mentioned how I subjectively cannot discover traces of a gender-related appeal in this sense. My impressions and memories may slightly change once I keep in mind visual representations of those singers, but what draws me to their voices is rather a quite elementary, perhaps "material" sense of bodily absorption.

The experience, on the other hand, that only masculine voices have a strong three-dimensional acoustic presence in my memory, in terms of their supportive and caring attitudes about my academic career, reflects institutional trajectories of education that are typical for men of my generation in Western cultures. Women of similar age would likely have less homogeneous recollections. In other words, if I observe any differences at all in my life between the functions of feminine and masculine voices, they all depend on existing social constellations connoted, recycled, and ultimately consolidated by them. Such functions, however, lie outside the lives of the voice. If more women associate the voice of conscience with a masculine than with a feminine tone, they of course project a gender-based social differential of power into the lives of their mind. We thus see how multiple, partly obvious and partly surprising phenomena come into view once we look at voice performance from the angle of gender difference. But these observations are too divergent for us to conclude that gender is a major component in the understanding of voices and their function for our existence. Rather I believe, with Nietzsche, that this function depends on an elementary level of materiality prior to social and even to most physical distinctions.

The sense of merging and becoming one with other bodies, however, as it often occurs while we are listening to beautiful singing voices, belongs to such primordial materiality and thus does not have any visual equivalent enabling us to easily imagine or even describe such "one-ness" in its form and substance. We don't sense a one-ness on the level of bodies and voices being Present-at-Hand, that is as objects of perception and experience. Nor is it a one-ness on the level of Ready-to-Hand where different bodies or voices would fulfill coordinated functions, as is the case with the different voices making up a choir. Being overwhelmed and becoming one with a voice, I believe, happens in a more primordial dimension of having a body, in a dimension corresponding to the elementary intuition and state of being material. Closeness in this dimension cannot be measured by shorter or larger distance; rather it is an affinity, or better, a contiguity with everything else that is matter, matter as occupying space and being palpable. Such closeness may be the fundamental reason why we like to say that we "can hold onto" voices that absorb and overwhelm us, although holding onto a voice is of course impossible in any literal sense. It may well be an elementary physical state, less fully functionalized in the case of humans than in that of animals whose instincts we interpret as perfectly adapted physical and thus material reactions to challenges from their environment. Being less instinct-oriented, we don't have a clear position for that materiality in our existence. It is always with us, although we can neither fully bracket nor fully embrace it.

If such materiality is the zone where the absorption of listeners through overwhelming voices happens, it may also be the reason for the astonishingly recurrent association of great popular singers with death that we have observed—not, of course, as a physical or as a pragmatic connection between death and great voices but in the form of two different plays of connotation. One play of connotation would be tautological, with death as pure matter affirming and emphasizing the material zone of fusion between humans that voices can sometimes produce. The other connotation functions by contrast and highlights voices as a condensation of life against death as its background. Such connotational plays have little to do with the structures or trajectories along which voice behavior unfolds. Rather we should interpret them as traces of an apprehension facilitated by the relation between the potentially overwhelming effects of great singing voices and the awareness of a non-functional materiality in human existence.

Our focus on situations where beloved voices produce not only an impression but the psycho-physical reality of being overwhelmed has taken us to a state of materiality within human existence that we always carry with us and that both precedes and permeates human culture—although neither our everyday languages nor the treatises of Western philosophy have distinctive concepts for it. Here I see the beginning of an answer to my central question of why it is impossible—and probably not only for me—to imagine life without favorite voices. They are matter not only by what they do to us in situations of precariousness but also—in the literal sense—as a medium of primary physical closeness shared by all humans. When we sense that we are matter, we never find ourselves completely alone or threatened by absolute discontinuity. On this ground, which hardly ever becomes a fully circumscribed reference or a meaning in our consciousness, voices can help us in precarious situations of individual life. To say that we "hold onto voices" may show the limits in our awareness and in our way of articulating such founding materiality.

As I have adapted my thoughts about the human voice to the voice's status of a "disorderly topic" by surrounding it with a series of analyses and arguments developed from different perspectives, I don't feel obliged to finish this disorderly essay on one ultimate point of convergence or on one major thesis. With the observation, however, of a primordial materiality[4] and closeness becoming almost literally palpable in the process of being overwhelmed by singing voices, a potential vanishing point for all our reflections has come into sight. With thoughts about overwhelming voices having brought that primordial materiality and closeness to our attention, we can retrospectively say that it was a presupposition and that it had a function in all the other situations I have been referring to as "lives of the voice." If being exposed to human voices always triggers elements in the imaginary that we then interiorize and accumulate on sensible layers of our personalities, we can indeed say that voices never operate without producing effects of fusion that imply our primary material existence.

As a premise, implication, and effect of any human activity, sheer materiality constitutes a transcendental horizon for our existence—not the horizon "above" human existence that religions have reserved for all kinds of "higher beings" but, so to speak, a transcendental horizon "below," a horizon of substance and grounding that we hardly ever think about. Perhaps religions have to deal with the relations between their gods and voices because this conceptual realm concerns the ontology of the separation or of the intersection between pure spirituality transcending life from above and pure materiality transcending life from below. Islam keeps its god at an infinite distance from the materiality-evoking voice; Christianity goes far in merging the two transcendental horizons through notions and narratives referring to the voice as a medium of incarnation; and

Judaism has a wide range of different possibilities to imagine the divine voice, thus endowing God with a more ambiguous—or more differentiated—ontology.

Whenever voices are part of our behavior, the transcendental horizon of materiality below human existence is drawing nearer. Voices therefore always function as unconcealment of our non-circumscribed closeness to other humans, of a closeness in which we live and in which we are materiality. But as philosophers mostly use the word "unconcealment" for situations and events where phenomena seem to fully show themselves, we need to differentiate its meaning based on the hope that to think about voices has at least been a way for that primary state of material closeness to develop in our mind—without fully revealing all its aspects and dimensions. Thinking about voices has pushed further the sense of closeness as an existential dimension—even if we only understand that concepts and arguments are not enough to grasp what is at stake with voices.

Gratitude for Intellectual Closeness . . .

. . . is on my mind, rather than the usual list of acknowledgments for timely moments of advice or critique, as I am finishing the revision of this book's manuscript. Different from most other projects that I have pursued over the past five decades, it has emerged from a fascination that seemed to be only mine and was thus necessarily remote from ongoing debates in the academic humanities and in the North American, South American, and European public spheres. The friends who reacted to my concentration on *Lives of the Voice* and to the subsequent chapters that I wrote did so in a spirit of openness and generosity that gave my intellectual solitude a horizon of unexpected liveliness. For years of attention and conversation, I would thus like to thank

VITTORIA BORSÓ, who reads the closest

ANDREA CAPRA, whom I am missing at Stanford's Coupa Café every Thursday morning

CHRISTEL BALTES-LÖHR, who is able to listen to academic writing

EVA GILMER, who trusted my brain and mind

GREICY PINTO BELLIN, who was at listening distance from Curitiba

EVA HIMO SAADEH, STEFANO PERPETUINI, SIYI QI, and above all ETAN HIRSH, who produced the energy of a much larger class at the Hebrew University

IRINA HRON and CHRISTIAN BENNE, who speak with the snow and the sun

JÉZIO HERNANI BOMFIM GUTIERRE, who looked over my shoulder without knowing

LEONHARD MÖCKL, whose Franconian voice has a cosmopolitan touch

OSLEI BEGA and GABRIEL LIMA LEAL, whose presence at Campo Grande was endless

MELANIE MÖLLER, who makes persuasion charming

MICHAEL ALBERT, whose conversation is part of all my intellectual concerns

BIRGIT MÜNCH and MARKUS GABRIEL, who gave "voice" the aura of a philosophical topic

THOMAS PAVEL, who shares an agnostic belief in voices of transcendence

LUDWIG PFEIFFER, whose preciseness inspires

BRIAN PINES, who said he enjoyed cold, early morning schedules

ANJA POMPE, who asks out of the blue

ANTONIO RAFELE, who opened a Ciceronian space for me

RICKY, whose voice is the center of my life

THAMARA RODRIGUES and MARCELO RANGEL, who didn't mind the rhythm of my prose

VICTOR MANUEL SÁNCHEZ, who talks philosophy while preparing cappuccinos

JAN SOEFFNER, whose voice I hear when I read him

MIGUEL TAMEN, who is my intellectual gold standard

ERICA WETTER, who encouraged me and yet remained patient

and GILL ZIMMERMANN, who heard me write on the upper floor

Notes

Chapter 1

1. Jacques Derrida, *La voix et le phénomène: Introduction au problème du signe dans la phénoménologie de Husserl* (Paris: Presses Universitaires de France, 1967).

2. Friedrich Kittler, *Musik und Mathematik. Band 1: Hellas / Teil 1: Aphrodite* (Munich: Wilhelm Fink, 2006).

3. Doris Kolesch and Sybille Krämer, eds., *Stimme: Annäherung an ein Phänomen* (Frankfurt am Main: Suhrkamp, 2006).

4. Roland Barthes, "Le grain de la voix" [1972], in *L'obvie et l'obtus: Essais critiques III* (Paris: Editions du Seuil, 1982), pp. 236–245.

5. This section draws from page 239 and following in "Le grain de la voix." Unless noted otherwise, all translations in the book are mine.

6. See, most notably, Hans Ulrich Gumbrecht, *Production of Presence: What Meaning Cannot Convey* (Stanford: Stanford University Press, 2004).

7. As director of nonfiction publications at Suhrkamp Verlag, Eva reacted with these words to my first drafts for this book, implying that disorderly topics deserve intellectual attention in spite of—or because of—their specific challenges.

8. In recent decades, philosophically complex proposals to solve the epistemological problem related to the concept of human life have come from the so-called life sciences rather than from the humanities. Such attempts often start out with long-term evolutionary overviews about the emergence of life in general, and of human life specifically, as a process with two thresholds of extremely high im-

probability. Two eminent examples for this approach are Lynn Margulis, Dorion Sagan, and Niles Eldredge, *What Is Life?* (New York: Simon & Schuster, 1998) and Carlo Rovelli, *The Order of Time* (New York: Riverhead Books, 2018).

Chapter 2

1. The following remarks are based on my book: Hans Ulrich Gumbrecht, *Atmosphere, Mood, Stimmung: On a Hidden Potential of Literature* (Stanford: Stanford University Press, 2012).

2. Paul Celan, "Stimmen," in *Sprachgitter* (Frankfurt: S. Fischer Verlag, 1961), pp. 7–9.

Chapter 3

1. Helmuth Plessner, *Lachen und Weinen: Eine Untersuchung der Grenzen menschlichen Verhaltens* [1941], in *Gesammelte Schriften VII: Ausdruck und menschliche Natur* (Frankfurt: Suhrkamp, 1982), pp. 201–387.

2. Friedrich Nietzsche, "12 = Mp XII 1 d. Frühjahr 1871," in *Sämtliche Werke. Kritische Studienausgabe in 15 Bänden,* vol. 7, edited by Herausgegeben von Giorgio Colli and Mazzino Montinari (Munich: Deutscher Taschenbuchverlag, 1980), pp. 359–369.

3. Originally coined by Antonin Artaud in the late 1940s, Gilles Deleuze first gave a philosophical development to this concept in his book *Logique du sens* (Paris: Éditions du Minuit, 1969).

Chapter 4

1. My reference is the German edition: Georg Wilhem Friedrich Hegel, *Phänomenologie des Geistes*, vol. 3 in *Werke in 20 Bänden (auf der Grundlage der Werke von 1832–1845 neu edierte Ausgabe*, edited by Eva Moldenhauer and Karl Markus Michel (Frankfurt: Suhrkamp, 1970), pp. 178–323, in particular, pp. 222 ff.

2. Above all, Karl-Heinz Göttert, *Geschichte der Stimme* (Munich: Wilhelm Fink, 1998), and Friedrich Kittler, Thomas Macho, and Sigrid Weigel, eds., *Zwischen Rauschen und Offenbarung, Zur Kultur- und Mediengeschichte der Stimme* (Berlin: De Gruyter, 2002).

3. Julia Fischer, "Tierstimmen," in *Stimme: Annäherung an ein Phänomen*, edited by Doris Kolesch and Sybille Krämer (Frankfurt am Main: Suhrkamp, 2006), pp. 171–190.

4. Charles Darwin, *Expressions of the Emotions in Man and Animals*, with preface by Margaret Mead (New York: Philosophical Library, 1955).

5. Darwin, *Expressions of the Emotions*, p. 90.

6. Darwin, *Expressions of the Emotions*, p. 87.

7. In the first volume of his monumental work *Sphären* (Frankfurt: Suhrkamp, 1998), Peter Sloterdijk reads the Sirens' episode (pp. 487–542) without distinguishing between their words and their "clear-toned song." According to him, the Sirens' temptation lies in the flattering reference to Odysseus's "glory."

8. I am referring to the third chapter of André Jolles, *Einfache Formen* (Halle: De Gruyter, 1930).

9. Irmgard Männlein-Robert, *Stimme, Schrift und Bild: Zum Verhältnis der Künste in der hellenistischen Dichtung* (Heidelberg: (Universitätsverlag Winter, 2007), p. 9. For my remarks on Greek and Roman antiquity, I mainly rely on the introductory chapters of this work and on Melanie Möller's outstanding book *Ciceros Rhetorik als Theorie der Aufmerksamkeit* (Heidelberg: Universitätsverlag Winter, 2013).

10. Aristotle, *De Anima*, Book II, Section 8.

11. I referred to the German translation of Aristotles's *Rhetoric* by Paul Gohlke (Paderborn: Ferdinand Schöningh, 1959), Book III, Section 1. The translation into English is mine.

12. I referred to the Latin-German edition of Marcus Fabius Quintilianus's *Institutiones Oratoriae—Libri XII*, edited and translated by Helmut Rahn (Darmstadt: Wissenschaftliche Buchgesellschaft, 1972). The translation into English is mine.

13. Männlein-Robert, *Stimme, Schrift und Bild*, p. 188.

14. Möller, *Ciceros Rhetorik als Theorie der Aufmerksamkeit*, pp. 320 ff.

15. For a discussion of some important aspects about voices in the Middle Ages (without an overarching thesis), see Irit Ruth Kleiman, ed., *Voice and Voicelessness in Medieval Europe: The New Middle Ages* (London: Palgrave Macmillan, 2015).

16. Song 3 (with the opening "Farei un vers de dreyt nien") is quoted from Frederick Goldin, trans., *Lyrics of the Troubadours and Trouvères* (Garden City: Anchor Books, 1973), pp. 24–26.

17. The ancient Provençal word for "song" is *vers*, exclusively referring to the prosodic form of the genre.

18. K. Ludwig Pfeiffer, "Operngesang und Medietheorie," in Kolesch and Krämer, *Stimme*, pp. 65–84.

19. See Reinhart Meyer-Kalkus, *Stimme und Sprechkünste im 20. Jahrhundert* (Berlin: Akademie Verlag, 2001), pp. 14 ff. Mainly dedicated to institutions of vocal performance during the past century, this book provides detailed knowledge about earlier treatises and debates concerning different functions of the voice.

20. François de la Rochefoucauld, *Oeuvres Complètes*. edited by Louis Martin-Chauffier (Paris: Bibliothèque de la Pléiade [Gallimard]), 1935), p. 249.

21. La Rochefoucauld, *Oeuvres Complètes, p. 255*.

22. Jean de la Bruyère, *Oeuvres Complètes*, edited by Julien Benda (Paris: Bibliothèque de la Pléiade [Gallimard], 1967).

23. La Bruyère, *Oeuvres Complètes*, p. 437.

24. La Bruyère, *Oeuvres Complètes*, p. 445.

25. La Bruyère, *Oeuvres Complètes*, p. 448.

26. La Bruyère, *Oeuvres Complètes*, p. 110.

27. The "animal scream of passion" is a motif appearing throughout Diderot's work. See Hélène Cussac, "The Vital Dynamism of the Voice in Diderot," *Etudes Epistémè* 29 (2016).

28. Regarding Goethe's voice fascination and related activities, see Meyer-Kalkus, *Stimme und Sprechkünste,* pp. 241 ff.

29. For details and some suggestive interpretations of this period in the history of technology, see Thomas Macho, "Stimmen ohne Körper: Anmerkungen zur Technikgeschichte der Stimme," in Kolesch and Krämer, *Stimme,* pp. 130–146.

30. See Román Gubern and Katleen M. Vernon, "Soundtrack," in *A Companion to Spanish Cinema,* edited by Jo Labanyi and Tatjana Pavlovid (Cambridge: Blackwell, 2012), pp. 370–388.

31. For Cassirer's ideas regarding the voice, see Meyer-Kalkus, *Stimme und Sprechkünste,* pp. 28 ff.

32. Meyer-Kalkus, *Stimme und Sprechkünste,* dedicates an entire chapter to Jünger's text (pp.193–212).

33. See Cornelia Epping-Jäger, "Stimmgewalt: Die NSDAP als Rednerpartei," in Kolesch and Krämer, *Stimme,* pp. 147–170.

34. Jünger seems to come back here to the admiring way in which many Germans had been referring to Goebbels by using his academic title.

35. Quoted in Meyer-Kalkus, *Stimme und Sprechkünste,* p. 210.

36. Dieter Mersch, "Präsens und Ethizität der Stimme," in Kolesch and Krämer, *Stimme,* pp. 211–236.

37. Bernhard Waldenfels, „Das Lautwerden der Stimme," in Kolesch and Krämer, *Stimme,* pp. 191–210.

Chapter 5

1. Jean-Paul Sartre, *L'Imaginaire: Psychologie Phénoménologique de l'Imagination* (Paris: Gallimard, 1940).

2. I am not aware of any critical discussions and subsequent systematic proposals about historical or current distinctions between the concepts "imagery," "imaginary," and "imagination." While "imagination" is normally connected to a capacity of the human mind, as opposed to "imagery" or "imaginary," referring to impressions that imagination can activate, the word "imagination" sometimes covers both dimensions. As for "imagery" and "imaginary," it is my impression that Anglo-American analytic thinkers have a preference for the former word, whereas Continental thinkers (following such different authorities as Jacques Lacan or Wolfgang Iser) prefer to use the latter. In this chapter I join the Continental tendency.

3. Wolfgang Iser, *The Fictive and the Imaginary: Charting Literary Anthropology* (Baltimore: Johns Hopkins University Press, 1993), pp. xvii, 234.

4. Mainly developed in Louis Hjelmslev, *Prolegomena to a Theory of Language* (Baltimore: University of Indiana Press, 1940).

5. Scholars consider imagination to be the central concept of concentration in the first stage of Lacan's work and seminars (1936–1953). His most notable association between the body and the imaginary refers exclusively to the visual dimension. It states that in the "mirror stage" in child development, the imaginary replaces the impression of a fragmented body with a form of wholeness.

6. Georg Christoph Lichtenberg, "Über Physiognomik; Wider die Physiognomen. Zur Beförderung der Menschenliebe und Menschenkenntnis," in *Schriften und Briefe,* vol. 3, edited by Wolfgang Promies. (Munich: Hanser Verlag, 1972), pp. 256–295. For the passage discussed, see pp. 284 ff.

7. About the inevitability of body imaginings based on the perception of voices and on their three-dimensionality, see Reinhart Meyer-Kalkus, *Stimme und Sprechkünste im 20. Jahrhundert* (Berlin: Akademie Verlag, 2001), p. 12.

8. See my essay, "Rhythmus und Sinn," in *Materialität der Kommunikation,* edited by Hans Ulrich Gumbrecht and Karl Ludwig Pfeiffer (Frankfurt: Suhrkamp, 1988), pp. 223–239. The English translation of the volume was published in 1992 by Stanford University Press.

9. In this passage I rely on the expertise of my friend and Stanford colleague Joshua Landy, one of the leading contemporary Proust scholars.

10. Julian Jaynes, *The Origin of Consciousness in the Breakdown of the Bicameral Mind* (Boston: Houghton Mifflin Company, 1976).

Chapter 6

1. By referring to the text of the Torah as the Old Testament, I follow the predominant (although not exclusive) custom among contemporary academics in Israel.

2. *The New Oxford Annotated Bible: New Revised Standard Version with the Apocrypha,* augmented 3rd ed. (Oxford: Oxford University Press, 2007).

3. I owe this philological insight to Etan Hirsh, who participated in my class "Lives of the Voice" at the Hebrew University, Jerusalem, in May 2023.

4. Quoting Etan Hirsh's outstanding paper for my "Lives of the Voice" seminar at the Hebrew University.

5. With this concept, I again follow Etan Hirsh's seminar paper. As the vanishing point of a philological argument, he demonstrates how in the Talmudic tradition individual words for religious or divine voice events sometimes yielded "two things, meaning and physicality"—which also shows how the oral presence of the Torah could "only understand as a dualism or a voice, what was originally one or a voice-thing." The observation may also help to understand why Talmudic debates quite regularly invoke *kol* as *bat kol*–that is, "the daughter of voice." In Genesis 4: 10 ff, by contrast, *kol* appears as a word with which God refers to the "voice" of Abel's blood who has been killed by his brother Cain: "Listen: your brother's blood is crying out to me from the ground! And now you are cursed from the ground, which has opened its mouth to receive your brother's blood from your hand." Invoking the "mouth" of the ground seems to support the understanding of *kol* as "voice-thing." I owe this textual observation to my friend Amir Eshel.

6. Most likely due to the non-theological connotations that the word "magical" normally evokes, Catholic theology refrains from using it in self-referential contexts.

7. *The Holy Qur'an, 15th ed.,* translated by Abdullah Yusuf Ali (New York: Tahrike Tarsile Qu'ran, 2005).

8. This well-established suspicion of self-complacency gives its unbearable ring of banality to the German proverb *"ein gutes Gewissen ist ein sanftes Ruhekissen"* ("good conscience is a soft cushion of peace").

9. Sigmund Freud, "Zur Einführung des Narzißmus," in *Gesammelte Werke: chronologisch geordne: Zehnter Band: Werke aus den Jahren 1913–1917* (Frankfurt: Fischer Taschenbuch Verlag, 1999), pp. 137–170, quote on p. 163.

10. *Stimmung*, the German word for mood, does not appear in this specific passage of *Being and Time*, but is analyzed here as a way to resist individual movements of agency and change later on in the book.

11. Martin Heidegger, *Being and Time*, translated by John Macquarrie and Edward Robinson (San Francisco: Harper & Co., 1962).

Chapter 7

1. Friedrich Nietzsche, "12 = Mp XII 1 d. Frühjahr 1871," in *Sämtliche Werke. Kritische Studienausgabe in 15 Bänden*, vol. 7, edited by Herausgegeben von Giorgio Colli and Mazzino Montinari (Munich: Deutscher Taschenbuchverlag, 1980), pp. 359–369.

2. Jon Pareles, "Pop Reviews: Part Divas, Part Goddesses: 2 Women of Glamour and Music; Whitney Houston at Radio City," *New York Times*, September 19, 1994. https://www.nytimes.com/1994/09/19/arts/pop-reviews-part-divas-part-goddesses-2-women-glamour-music-whitney-houston.html

3. "The 200 Greatest Singers of All Time: 2 Whitney Houston," *Rolling Stone*, January 1, 2023. https://www.rollingstone.com/music/music-lists/best-singers-all-time-1234642307/whitney-houston-11-1234643211/

4. A materiality more elementary indeed than the one evoked by the contributions to the volume edited by Karl Ludwig Pfeiffer and myself: *Materialität der Kommunikation* (Frankfurt: Suhrkamp, 1988), and its then emerging focus on media.

The authorized representative in the EU for product safety and compliance is:
Mare Nostrum Group B.V.
Mauritskade 21D
1091 GC Amsterdam
The Netherlands
Email address: gpsr@mare-nostrum.co.uk

KVK chamber of commerce number: 96249943

www.ingramcontent.com/pod-product-compliance
Lightning Source LLC
LaVergne TN
LVHW051818060925
820435LV00002B/19

* 9 7 8 1 5 0 3 6 4 2 4 8 5 *